PRESENTING
YOUR
RESEARCH

SUCCESS IN RESEARCH

The Success in Research series has been designed by Cindy Becker and Pam Denicolo to provide short, authoritative and accessible guides for students, researchers and academics on the key area of professional and research development.

Each book is written with an eye to avoiding jargon and each aims to cut to the chase of what readers really need to know about a given topic. These are practical and supportive books and will be essential reading for any students or researchers interested in developing their skills and broadening their professional and methodological knowledge.

SUCCESS IN RESEARCH

PRESENTING YOUR RESEARCH

CONFERENCES, SYMPOSIUMS, POSTER PRESENTATIONS AND BEYOND

LUCINDA BECKER

⑤SAGE

Los Angeles | London | New Delhi
Singapore | Washington DC

Los Angeles | London | New Delhi
Singapore | Washington DC

SAGE Publications Ltd
1 Oliver's Yard
55 City Road
London EC1Y 1SP

SAGE Publications Inc.
2455 Teller Road
Thousand Oaks, California 91320

SAGE Publications India Pvt Ltd
B 1/I 1 Mohan Cooperative Industrial Area
Mathura Road
New Delhi 110 044

SAGE Publications Asia-Pacific Pte Ltd
3 Church Street
#10-04 Samsung Hub
Singapore 049483

Editor: Katie Metzler
Editorial assistant: Lily Mehrbod
Production editor: Thea Watson
Copy-editor: Neil Dowden
Proofreader: Bryan Campbell
Marketing manager: Ben Griffin-Sherwood
Cover design: Shaun Mercier
Typeset by: C&M Digitals (P) Ltd, Chennai, India
Printed in Great Britain by Henry Ling Limited at
The Dorset Press, Dorchester, DT1 1HD

Library of Congress Control Number: 2013946899

British Library Cataloguing in Publication data

A catalogue record for this book is available from
the British Library

MIX
Paper from
responsible sources
FSC
www.fsc.org   FSC™ C013985

ISBN 978-1-4462-7588-7
ISBN 978-1-4462-7589-4 (pbk)

CONTENTS

ABOUT THE AUTHOR

Dr Lucinda Becker, an award-winning Associate Professor in the Department of English Literature at the University of Reading, University Teaching Fellow and Senior Fellow of the Higher Education Academy, has spent her career committed to enhancing the skills and knowledge of undergraduates and research postgraduates. She has written numerous successful study skills guides for students. As a professional trainer she also works throughout the United Kingdom and Europe, devising and delivering training in communication and management techniques, principally to lawyers, engineers and scientists.

One

INTRODUCTION

Working as part of a community is the lifeblood of academia and, indeed, of most commercial organisations. Although there will be times, perhaps most of your time, spent working alone on a project, if you cannot stand up and present your findings, in one form or another, you will struggle to achieve the intellectual and professional success which will allow you to move on to even more interesting projects. Being seen to present success-fully is part of being successful in professional and academic settings alike; this is something you need to get right. This sounds a little dramatic, so for a moment I will consider with you what might be gained from presenting:

1. You can test out your theories on like-minded people, to see what they think.
2. Just as importantly, you are testing out your hypotheses – and your material – on yourself. By speaking out loud you will find that your thoughts crystallise: if something does not sound quite right, it will become clear to you as you prepare to speak.
3. You will receive encouragement from your peers. I am always pleased to be reminded of how generous audiences are: they really do want you to do well.
4. You will be gaining valuable feedback on the specifics of your work. This is the most obvious benefit to be taken from presenting your research and it should never be underestimated (even if, at times, it can be a little challenging).
5. Unlike a publication, the feedback you receive is in 'real time': as you present your findings, so you get an immediate response. Reviews of a publication are quite a different thing: at that stage there is nothing you can do to change your published words.
6. Presenting allows you to take a break from your day-to-day activity as a researcher. This may sound minor, but it can be hugely important in prac-tice. In taking a break from your everyday research life, you are allowing

some intellectual fresh air into your mind: great thoughts often appear on the train to or from an event.

7. You will be showered with ideas, references and resource information as you present. This can be a little bewildering the first time you do it, but every lead someone gives you will represent hours of detective work which you now no longer have to do. You need to see yourself as a research honey-bee, gathering as much helpful information as you can before you return to the hive to ponder on it.

8. You will learn about the money. Which grants are being offered, which of your fellow scholars are grouping together to bid for funding in an area where you could also collaborate, which funding body is thought to be turning towards an area in which you work, which universities are hiring lecturers, and so on. This information may well not be available in print at the time of the event, so you are ahead of the game simply by being there.

9. You will be raising your professional profile by presenting. For most scholars, most of the time, funding (either in the form of a research grant or a job as an academic) is going to be key to their continued research, and the esteem in which it is held, so recognising this aspect of presenting is crucial.

10. There is one final benefit to be had, which is pure pleasure: feeling that you are part of a community, and that is where I will begin …

Becoming part of the general community of scholars or professionals and, more especially, becoming part of your own particular niche group, does not happen overnight, nor is it achieved without effort. However, the effort is undoubtedly worth it. I recall the first conference at which I gave a paper. I was terrified – far more terrified than I had expected – and was hardly sure about how I was going to get through the half hour that my paper would take. I did get through it, but rather badly, I thought. I blushed terribly throughout, read the paper with relatively little expression, answered the questions which the audience members posed and frantically made notes as they offered help. It took perhaps six months for me to realise fully how wonderful the occasion had been. I was still, even after so many months, looking up and using the material which had been mentioned by the audience; I had dropped a whole planned chapter of my Master's dissertation because, in the light of the comments made, I could now see that it would not fit with my central hypothesis; I had gone back and corrected a false assumption I had made, which a fellow scholar (who later became a good friend and mentor) had gently pointed out as erroneous.

I had approached this first presentation with entirely the wrong view. I had seen it as a test of nerves, I had seen myself as offering the fruits of my research to a passive audience of recipients and I had done all of this with both trepidation and a slight resentment that the conference organiser (who was my supervisor – how could I refuse?) had dragged me from my happy seclusion and asked me to share my precious, private research ideas.

As you can see, I did not face my first experience of presenting my research with anything like equanimity, but I came to understand that it had been an entirely positive move to make. You might not, of course, be feeling anything like as scared as I was, and your approach could be very different to the one I took, so perhaps we should introduce ourselves a little, at least in terms of presenting research.

My research specialism, back when I gave that first paper, was Early Modern women, death and dying. I was looking mainly at the 1590s to the 1640s and I was considering how women approached the test of 'dying well' (an important concept at that time) and how, once dead, they might be refigured publically to have been the 'perfect woman', whatever the reality of their lives. From this starting point I went in many different directions in my research, including seeing death, in a rather strange way, as an opportunity for a woman to have her writings published.

At the time of giving the paper I was already a professional trainer (mainly in the technical and scientific professions) and had taught at various levels, so I considered myself to have some expertise. I am not sure that this helped me hugely when faced with that conference, but what has always stayed with me (literally, in the case of some of my peers) was the fact that, by the end of the conference – for which, unwittingly, I wore a black dress – I was nicknamed 'the death woman' amongst several scholars. As my interest in the field grew, and my passion for my subject deepened, the fact that I was termed, in some quarters, the death woman, opened many doors for me. People recognised me when I emailed them, at conferences scholars would come up and start talking to me straight away about my subject area, I would receive advice and references to useful material – and all because I was cajoled into giving a presentation at a conference so early on in my academic career.

You may not be at such an early stage in your career; indeed, your career might not be in academia at all, but I think that I can surmise some things about you. You might simply be thinking about giving a presentation or contributing to a poster conference at some point, but it is more likely that this challenge is growing imminent. You might have some experience of presenting, either professionally or in a more social setting, but you feel you need to know more about what it is like to present to your peers in your current field of expertise. You might be facing your first presentation as a researcher or young professional. You might already have bought one of the books in this series and so feel that you can trust what you will find here.

There are obviously some variables in our acquaintance so far, but what I can know about you, without any doubt, is that you are concerned to get it right, that you are committed to your professional life and that you want to save yourself some time and anxiety by learning more about presenting before you face your next (which might, perhaps, be your first) presentation. With these variables in mind, there are several ways in which you could use this book:

1. If you have yet to give a presentation, but the prospect is looming, you would probably find it beneficial to read through the book in its entirety.
2. Once you begin to focus down on a presentation which you are planning to give, it would be worth tackling each chapter as you prepare: the guide has been designed to take you step by step through the process.
3. Once you have given the paper, or presented at a poster conference, you might return to the book to reread those chapters on areas where you think you might be able to improve next time.
4. If you have given professional presentations in the past, but not in your current role, you might want to read the book 'out of order', concentrating first on those areas where you are most interested to see the differences between different types of presentation.
5. For the reader who has more experience in presenting, the book could be used as a 'spot guide' to help fix those aspects of presenting which have been a particular challenge in the past.

Whichever way you choose to use the advice offered here, you will find exercises, checklists and top tips to help you as you progress.

Two

WHEN AND WHERE SHOULD I GIVE A PAPER?

There are two aspects to considering when to give a conference paper: chronological time and research time. Chronological time takes into account your workload, the time of year at which the conference is being held, the travelling involved in getting to the conference and the demands upon your time in the weeks leading up to the event. If you are a researcher rather than a professional, then research time will also be important. Research time would involve contemplating the intellectual prompts to action, such as where you are in your research endeavours, the opinion of your supervisor, and how ready you feel to emerge from your research hive and offer some of your findings to others.

Two answers often seem to emerge in response to the question of timing: either 'I do not have the time' (regardless of the actual circumstances) or 'How hard can it be? Of course I have the time!' (which is to ignore the commitment required for the task ahead). Neither of these is a realistic or accurate response, because it lacks any reflection upon the realities of the situation. What is more worrying is a researcher simply saying 'Well, I have to do it so I will', which is to dismiss, under pressure, the need to take into account either chronological or research time.

In deciding whether now is the right time to go ahead with a presentation of some sort, you might want to use this checklist:

 CHECKLIST

1 Do I have something to present? This might be an essay or report which could be reworked, a draft chapter of a dissertation or thesis, or an idea or area of research which you feel would fit nicely into a presentation slot.

(Continued)

(Continued)

2 Is it genuinely reworkable? We will consider later the advantages and pitfalls of reworking extant material against the challenges of starting from scratch for a presentation.
3 Is there an event for which this material would be a good fit?
4 Does that event require a mode of delivery which suits me? This might be simply reading a paper aloud, or delivering a more dynamic presentation of your material, or being part of a discussion panel, or giving a poster presentation. All of these options, and their pros and cons, will be considered later.
5 Do I feel ready to give a presentation? For some scholars the answer to this feels like it will always be 'no', but you can work up to a full-blown conference presentation by tackling smaller challenges first, and this guide will help you in doing this.
6 Is this the right time in my research life?
7 Is this the right time in my career?
8 Will this conference work well for me in chronological time?

I will be unpicking all of these options with you in this guide, so you may well return to this checklist later.

The last question in the checklist is the one I would like to consider with you first because, unlike the other points, it does not relate to your development as a researcher and presenter, but rather is concerned with the practicalities of your day-to-day life. When you are considering a conference it is a good idea to ignore, in the first instance, all of the intellectual or professional promptings to attend, and simply focus for a moment on the practicalities. The easiest way to do this, for most people, is to produce a 'personalised timetable' of the months leading up to the conference which is tempting you. If you have no specific conference in mind, making a timetable will help you identify gaps in your activities when you could afford the time to attend a conference, and this might help you in your search for the best event for you.

How you construct your personalised timetable is up to you, but I have included an example here of the type of timetable which would work in this context. I am assuming throughout this period that normal everyday tasks are being carried out, but you could add other rows such as 'reading', 'planning', 'supervisions' and so forth so as to offer yourself even more detail as you make your decision.

We can look at this timetable in a little more detail, imagining that it is your timetable:

- **February:** The research paper may, or may not, cover material which is suitable for the conference, but it would give you the chance to test some of the material with an audience and hopefully boost your presentation confidence. Teaching would take up much of your time this month, so giving the paper

	February	March	April	May	June	July	August	September
Research	Research seminar paper		Review panel		Draft Chapter 3 done			Supervisor meeting
Teaching	Full	Full					Summer School	Plan for new term
Earning						Job	Job	
Life				Two-week holiday				Birthday
Conference	Call for papers		Send synopsis/abstract		Plan		Write and prepare	Attend conference

would be your main research focus. However, you would still be able to keep an eye out for calls for papers, or be able to take a few minutes now and then to check online to see what is coming up. You notice a call for papers which suits you and your area of research, and choose to make this timetable.

- **March:** Here your month is also busy with teaching, and you would probably have the added workload of marking, so although you ponder the conference now and then, and perhaps make a few notes of what you might include in your synopsis, you would plan to do nothing more than that.

- **April:** Although your review panel appearance would take up much of your intellectual 'head space', you know that you need to get your synopsis or abstract for the conference sent off this month, so as to meet the deadline. Planning in advance like this allows you to make considered decisions about using the resources available to you, such as the academics on your review panel. You could take the opportunity to show them your synopsis or abstract for the conference and ask for their opinion, both of your idea for a paper and about whether that particular conference would be a good one to choose to showcase your work. You might, quite understandably, feel a little hesitant about sharing your conference plans at an event when you already feel under scrutiny, but it would be worth it. It is only by sharing your plans for dissemination that you can get the advice and feedback that you need; indeed, this is true of every form of dissemination of research.

- **May:** You would be pleased that you planned to this level of detail when May arrives. There are just routine research activities to carry out, perhaps some 'tidying up' of your research material, and then it is two glorious weeks of holiday. Of course, like most academics you would struggle not to take your academic mind on holiday with you, and you are bound to think about the challenge of the conference from time to time, but it is far enough away that you would, hopefully, take a proper break. Your research would be all the better for it.

- **June:** We all know that a rest helps productivity, so you would feel ready on your return to tackle the biggest month in the timetable. You have challenged yourself to complete a draft chapter of your thesis or dissertation, and you are also aiming to plan the conference paper. This is fortuitous timing in that you can arrange to see your supervisor to work through the draft chapter and the conference plan at the same meeting, but this is 'crunch month' as far as the conference is concerned. Writing up the paper is going to be a challenge, of course, but planning it out is often more demanding, so be ready for this in your timetable.

- **July:** As you would be busy earning money this month, it has been left free for you to focus on that, rather than distracting you or adding stress to your life by trying also to write a conference paper. If you have any leeway over your hours, you would probably try to work longer hours in July than in August, so as to give yourself a little extra time in August to write the paper, but this would not be a major factor in your decision making.

- **August:** This seems like a hugely busy month, and it is, with a week-long summer school at which you are teaching, and your vacation job, and writing up the conference paper. This is all perfectly possible, and you would not need to pull out of any of these commitments, but because you have planned so far in advance you might have been able to organise your research activities in such a way that this is fairly much a month away from new areas of research; your focus is outward facing throughout the month.

- **September:** The reason why 'write and prepare' rather than just 'write' was noted in August is that you need to make time not just to write the paper and/or prepare your presentation, but also to rehearse and revise it. By doing this well before the conference, you will be in a position this month simply to have one or two last-minute rehearsals before the event. These will reassure you that you have a convincing argument to make, and will present it well, without taking up too much of your time. You know that the new academic year is going to bring new teaching challenges; you also have a major meeting with your supervisor to plan the next stage in your research; the family celebration for your birthday will be a pleasure but also a drain on time. Thank goodness you planned this well!

I have produced an artificial timetable here, where the conference just happens to fall at the right stage of the year, but the principles remain the same regardless of your own circumstances: plan at least six months ahead, if you can, and spread the workload of the conference if possible. Of course, we have all heard of scholars who enjoy the adrenalin rush of writing their paper on the train on the way to the conference; you have probably even heard colleagues tell you that they are happy to improvise on the conference platform and prepare just a few brief notes. These are splendid anecdotes, but for most of us that simply would not work.

You will have different details in your timetable, and you may choose to have additional columns, but if you can it would make sense to try to follow the pattern of this timetable with regard to the conference. You will notice that, of the eight months covered here, there are five months in which activity relating to the conference is taking place, and three fallow months, in which the researcher has the chance to take a break from the conference preparation. Naturally, this will not mean taking a break from thinking about the conference, and that is largely the point of the fallow months. When you are not actually planning, writing or rehearsing, you are, inevitably, thinking about the event from time to time. This is often super-productive time: the moment in the shower when you suddenly think of a brilliant opening gambit; the lazy train journey during which you get a better feeling for the overall shape of your conference contribution; the moments before sleep when you recall a photograph which would be the perfect image to illustrate one of your points. If you possibly can, allow this spread of time in your planning: it usually pays dividends.

A personalised timetable such as this would take you through the months leading up to the conference. A word here about the week of the conference might be useful. Another checklist for you to consider:

CHECKLIST

During the week of the presentation event:

1 Do not give your paper to anyone else for them to check it for you – any feedback you get now will probably be too late to be useful and could sap your confidence.
2 Make sure that you have made back-ups for any visual material you are producing – data projectors can fail, for example.
3 Eat well and get to bed early on the penultimate night before the event – this is the night's sleep which will really make a difference to how you cope.
4 If you are asked to take on any additional work (more teaching, a new research activity, a team event), ask for a few days to think about it – you might miss a good opportunity if you simply say 'no' because you are under immediate pressure.
5 Check and double check the timing, the journey, the accommodation – all of the practicalities of the event – a week before the conference, to avoid any last-minute panics or problems on the day.
6 Plan your rehearsal schedule well. The main rehearsals will have happened the month before – restrict yourself to just one or two brief runs through this week.

I have covered aspects of your chronological time, but research time is also important. Listen to the promptings of those around you, and of your own research, to tell you when you should take the step towards presenting at a conference. You will probably already be aware that academic networking and raising your profile could both be useful in terms of your career goals (more on academic networking later in this guide), but your supervisor or mentor might not want to push against what seems to be a closed door. If you have never shown any interest in presenting your research, or if you have ever shared your doubts or fears about doing this, your supervisor/mentor might be loath to push you too hard. If you have made a commitment in your own mind to presenting your research in some way (and buying this book suggests that you have), then let your supervisor/mentor, and anyone else who could help, know that this is your position. At the very least it will allow them to keep you up to date with conferences they have heard about, or colloquia/symposia that they regularly attend.

The quiet promptings of your research can be difficult to discern. If you have embarked on a long-term project it is only natural that your focus will be on the final product (the thesis, project report or dissertation, for example). This can lead to you assuming that none of your work is ready for dissemination until this final stage, even though it might be. An audit of your work every few months makes sense here. Just taking an hour out of your everyday activities to see whether any of your work could be hived off and worked up into a paper or presentation could lead to surprising results. I will be asking you to consider later the types of material which might work for a conference contribution, but at this stage it is worth mentioning that a conference paper is not always (and, some would argue, not ever) the same as a thesis/dissertation chapter or section of a report. Audit your material not with an eye to its final published or submitted shape, but in smaller portions, any of which might work well as a conference offering.

I have been talking so far about papers and/or presentations, and later in this guide I will be discussing the different forms of conference presentation that are available to you, but before we move on I would like to consider, in broad terms, the types of conference which are open to you. It is often the case that a new researcher or young professional will leap at the first chance to present which offers itself. This is sometimes the result of fear ('I must just jump in and have a go at this') but it is more often a natural tendency to see the title of a conference and ignore the *mode* of the conference. Taking a moment now to consider this will allow you to make the best possible choice.

If we are to assume (and we can safely assume here) that there will be many conferences over the course of time which could fit your area of expertise, then we can focus on other important factors. When you see a 'call for papers', which might come to you either as an online alert or email, or from spotting a notice, you will naturally consider first the topic areas of the conference, but remember also that this is effectively a sales pitch for the event. The organisers are trying to persuade some scholars to give papers and other scholars to attend the conference. In making a decision you will want to find out a little more, before you commit, such as:

- Who is organising the event?
- What is it being called?
- What is the likely composition of the audience?
- Where is it being held?
- Who is funding it?
- Are the speakers' expenses being paid?
- Are there plans to publish the contributions?
- Are copies of the papers to be distributed in advance?
- What format will the event use?

Each of these factors may affect your decision as to whether or not to contribute to a conference, and I will be returning to them during the course of this book, but for now I will give a brief overview of why each of these factors could be important to you in the earliest stages of your planning.

Who is organising the event?

Conferences might be organised by postgraduate researchers, in which case they may primarily appeal to other postgraduate researchers as speakers (although this is not always the case). This would offer you a supportive atmosphere, but might not feel that different from a research seminar in your own institution. If it is being held elsewhere you could make useful contacts in your field; if it is being held in your own institution it would still count as useful practice and it would help you to network with academics beyond your immediate supervisory team.

Of course, it would be perfectly possible for you to arrange your own conference. This sounds like rather a lofty ambition, perhaps, but there are often good support systems in place (both practical and financial) to help those scholars who would like to arrange a conference, and naturally it would boost your prestige to have done such a thing.

What is it being called?

Various names are used for collective academic events. Symposia and colloquia (symposium and colloquium in the singular) may have academics giving papers, or may rely on 'round-table' discussions, or panel presentations. They are intended, usually, to be a little less rigid and formal than a full conference. If it is a conference, you would need to check on how the organisers expect material to be presented (more on that later in this guide). If the event is being termed a 'poster conference' you can be sure that creating a poster will be part of the event for most participants, but you might just check on that: sometimes they also have a few speakers without posters. If you are expected to give a poster, you would need to check whether it is simply a poster for viewing, or whether you will be standing beside it answering questions, or perhaps be required to give a brief presentation on your poster. If you are asked to give a paper at a 'research seminar' you would naturally assume that this is a relatively informal gathering, but it is still worth checking the other points on the list, just to confirm that it will be as casual you expect it to be.

What is the likely composition of the audience?

The size of the audience need not sway you unduly. It sounds far more terrifying to give a paper to an audience of 60 than to a group of six, yet most experienced presenters will confirm that the reverse is actually true. Of course, if it is an international conference with 500 in the audience you have the right to feel a little more nervous, but again it should not put you off. What is far more relevant to your decision making is the composition of the audience, and you can work this out, to some extent, by the breadth of the topic areas to be covered and the tone of the publicity. If it is a broad conference area, or a niche area which is just a little outside your field, you would expect to receive a broad range of questions, some of which might be quite challenging as non-experts try to assess your research position. A conference whose organisers clearly intend for it to be the 'gold standard' in its field, with high-profile speakers announced with the call for papers, for example, may be more demanding in terms of dovetailing your material to particular themed areas. A conference which falls exactly into your specialism is going to be valuable in terms of your research network.

Where is it being held?

Naturally you will take into account practicalities such as whether the conference is in your own country or abroad, but you might also like to think about your future plans in the context of location. If you know that you would relish the chance to work in your field at a particular university or other organisation, then you might want to present a paper there regardless of the inconvenience and/or expense. It is also worth asking around or putting up a notice if you are considering a conference at some distance from home: lift shares are common enough to make it worth your while to do this.

It is possible that the event at which you are thinking of presenting is not 'being held' in any traditional sense at all: webinars are a possibility. What webinars lack in terms of flexibility they can make up for in terms of accessibility, so if you are working in a remote geographic area this might be an avenue worth pursuing.

Are there confirmed speakers already?

If there are no named speakers at the time that the call for papers goes out, this need not put you off. Named speakers whose work you admire will always be an attraction, of course, but not having speakers advertised in advance can be a deliberate attempt on the part of the organisers to be as broadly welcoming to speakers and topic areas as possible.

Are the speakers' expenses being paid?

Practice here varies hugely, depending on who is funding the conference, where it is in the world and the traditions (and financial position) of the hosting organisation. If you need to be paid as a speaker in order to be there, ask about this early on. If the organisers are not paying expenses, but you are very keen to go, see if your own institution could help. Many organisations have a 'travel fund' or 'research dissemination fund' or something similar, which will contribute towards travel costs for those of their number who are delivering papers.

Are there plans to publish the contributions?

This could be the make or break decision moment for you. A publication as a result of a conference contribution is a gift to any academic. Sometimes conference organisers will have arranged in advance to bring out a special issue of a journal as a result of the conference, and plan to include every conference paper in there. Sometimes a book deal will have been made to produce a collected edition comprising selected conference papers. You might also hear that one of the delegates at the conference is planning something similar. Whilst you will not want to turn down a perfect call for papers just because there are no publication plans, if you were deciding between two conferences, this might be a key deciding factor.

Are copies of the papers to be distributed in advance?

This might seem like a minor detail four months ahead of the event, but four weeks before the conference, when you are being chased for a copy of your paper so that it can be circulated in advance to delegates, you might rue the day you agreed to this. As long as you have planned everything out, as I suggested earlier, this will not be a problem, but it is well worth checking at the outset whether this is a requirement. If it is, you will also want to ask about delivery: are delegates simply going to be asking questions about your paper, which they have all read in advance, or will you still be required to give the paper in some way at the event? Neither of these need be a problem, but you do need to know in advance.

What format will the event use?

Again, this information is not automatically included in a call for papers, but the format might play a role in your decision making. If, for example, you want to contribute to a conference but feel that a full-blown paper is beyond the reach of your time or your material at the moment, then a conference which includes panel or round-table discussions might be for you; if you want to be involved so as to gain some experience, but feel that a 'speaking part' is not for you yet, then a poster conference might be your best option. Before you dismiss a conference from your plans, it makes sense to consider the variety of ways in which the conference system can benefit you at each stage of your progression.

Working through the variables like this will, I hope, have given you a clearer sense of your options in terms of the standard forms of event at which you might present. Before we leave this area, however, we should consider other, less obvious avenues. If you are hoping to gain more confidence in public speaking before embarking on conferences, or if you would like to disseminate your research as widely as possible, there are other options open to you, such as:

- workshops
- toolbox talks
- public talks.

Workshops: these are usually thought of as teaching and learning events, rather than principally for disseminating research, but they can serve this purpose. If your area of expertise falls into a field which might be of more general interest, either to other academics or to a wider group of people, you might want to think about workshops as an option. They will give you some practice in standing up and talking about your research, but will not carry with them the formality of a conference paper; they allow others to question your research outcomes, but in a supportive environment; they require you to think on your feet, but in a way that is fluid and not too constraining.

If this idea appeals to you as, perhaps, a step on the road to a conference paper, contact those who might be interested in helping you to arrange such an event (your HR department, or the skills training section of your organisation, or managers of departments). Alternatively, check online with broad search terms around your area of expertise to see if there are already events happening elsewhere to which you could contribute as a workshop leader.

Toolbox talks: this term is sometimes used to describe lunchtime events during which members of an organisation can talk about their work, or their research into an area of work. If you are being funded by an employer for your research you may be obliged to give these talks as part of your funding package; if you are working as a professional they could be an optional part of your work life; if you are carrying out research which is not related to your working life, significant benefits can result from toolbox talks on your 'other life'.

Toolbox talks are not necessarily informal, but they are usually quite brief. They give you the chance to practise all of the presentation techniques you would use at a conference, but in a less daunting situation. Such is the popularity of these talks within professional circles that they are increasingly being used within academia, too, with research students joining with their supervisors/mentors and other academics to share experience and ideas around areas of mutual interest.

Public talks: these may sound like the opposite of a good way to ease yourself into the limelight, but in fact they can be very productive. Their availability to you might be limited, depending upon your area of expertise, but it is a good idea to take some time every now and then to look around you and see what is happening in the world outside your university or immediate workplace. Science and literary festivals abound nowadays, and most local societies regularly invite guest speakers to their meetings, so be creative and think about how you might 'break the ice' on introducing your material to the wider world in this way.

Three

CALLS FOR PAPERS: HOW THE CONFERENCE SYSTEM WORKS

It would be so refreshing if this bit of life were as simple as the title of this chapter suggests: 'calls for papers' would go out to every person who could in any conceivable way be interested in contributing to a conference, and those whose expertise perfectly matched the theme and topic areas of a conference would submit an abstract or synopsis, asking to present. Of course, life is never that simple; indeed, even the terminology can be off-putting for those without experience. Experienced academics know that a 'call for papers' is the stage in the process of arranging a conference when the theme and, often, some topic areas (however loosely defined) have been decided upon and now speakers are required to populate the conference. It may be that some illustrious 'keynote speakers' (those who will give the opening/closing papers for a session or for the whole conference) have been engaged, so that their names can be used on the publicity material to draw in more speakers. It may also be the case that the structure of the day (such as the division between single papers, groups of papers, panel or round-table discussions and so forth) has also been decided, which would allow the organisers to call for certain types of papers.

I enjoy the phrase 'call for papers' – it has a certain archaic ring to it and suggests, to my mind, a community of scholars being called to action. Others find it rather irritating, but it is used most commonly to invite submissions so it is worth adding it to your mental alert vocabulary as you wander corridors or browse online. One question might spring to your mind at this point: apart from wandering, either physically or online, how else might you break into the conference system?

This is a question over which I pondered for many weeks as a research student. I saw the odd notice, but was not sure whether it would be thought appropriate for me simply to submit a proposal for a conference contribution. I reassured myself that my enthusiastic and supportive supervisor would let me know when she thought I was ready. If only she had. This attitude meant several more weeks wondering how I could prove my readiness for this next step in my academic career, and trying to work out what I was doing so wrong that she did not yet consider me at the right stage to present any of my research. In the end I steeled myself to face her and ask what I was doing wrong. The simple answer was 'nothing', but the fact that she was so enthusiastic and supportive had led us to be at cross-purposes. Her enthusiasm meant that she could not imagine anyone not asking about conferences if they were so keen to go to one, whilst her supportive side had made her hold back from suggesting that I might think about it, just in case I could not afford the expense of attending a conference, or did not feel ready yet.

I have discovered since then that this is a common problem. Supervisors and mentors hesitate to thrust you forward into the world of presenting, whilst you remain unsure of what this is saying about your abilities and achievements so far. Add to this the complexities of the system, and you have a recipe for confusion and disappointment. The simplest answer to the problem is, of course, simply to be bold and ask. If you feel shy about suggesting straight off that you want to present, you could begin the conversation by asking for information about any conferences of which your supervisor/mentor has heard, with the idea that you might attend. That gives your supervisor the chance to recommend that you present, and if the recommendation is not forthcoming you could return to the topic once you have found out a little more about the conference and assured yourself that it is one at which you would like to present.

So, how do you find out about conferences in your area of interest? There are several ways to stay in the loop:

In person: In the ideal world you might see yourself casually dropping the topic of conferences into conversation, to be met with an excited chatter of ideas and information about the perfect event at which you could present your material. In reality it is far better to take a targeted approach to this. Make a commitment to yourself, right now, that you will spend the next week asking your peers and supervisor/mentors about conferences and similar events. Have a notebook ready and make sure you capture all of the information: some of it will be a vague mention of, for example, a research group who told someone that they might be arranging a symposium at the end of their project, so you will need to do a bit of digging to firm up vague data.

If you are at an early stage of thinking about dissemination through conferences, symposia and such like, it is fine if you would prefer to tell people, if they ask, that you have not yet decided exactly when you will be ready to give a paper. At the least you will get some feedback from them about their view of when you might be ready to take the next step; you will also have put yourself forward as someone who is interested in this for the future, so the chances are that they will keep you in mind the next time they come across conference details that they are asked to pass on to colleagues.

One-off conferences are, of course, common, but they also come in series. If a research project is due to take three of four years, and especially if it is being carried out by a group comprising scholars from across several institutions, there is likely to be a series of academic events being held throughout the project. In the formative stages of the project these could be sharing events (symposia, colloquia and similar) designed to offer tentative research findings and to draw other scholars into the field of activity (either simply to raise academic interest or practically, if more researchers are needed on the project). Towards the end of the project there are likely to be summative events, such as single presentations or much larger conferences. The opportunities for you here are wide, but these projects tend to be mentioned in person and in passing, so be alert to anything you hear and check it out online as soon as you can. Subscribe to the mailing list of any projects which are relevant to your area of interest, or make a 'conference favourites' group online so that you can check on their activity regularly.

In hard copy: It might sound a little old-fashioned, but notices and flyers are still popular and might help you to find something which could elude you online. This will mean, though, that you need to stroll around several departments of your institution or organisation, so as to make sure that you do not overlook inter-disciplinary opportunities for dissemination. If a friend or colleague is attending a conference in your area of interest, ask for copies of any conference flyers which are given out there.

By email: If you have an email address group you regularly use for sharing ideas and gaining inspiration (effectively, an 'online brainstorm group'), make sure that they all know you are interested in presenting your material. You could also try www.conferencealerts.com. Registration is currently free and the organisation will send you email alerts about events which fit the criteria you enter onto the system when you register.

Online: Any search for conferences in your area of interest is easy enough, but take it further than this. Rather than simply using search terms around your research or professional focus, try also entering the name of any researchers (perhaps their name + conference as a search term) whose books you have enjoyed. Those who write well often speak well and if you have come across an inspiring research text it can add to the momentum you gain from it to hear the writer in person. It might also allow you to hear about the next stage in that writer's academic journey, and to learn about research which is not yet published. It might even be the factor that moves you from planning to attend a conference to deciding to present at it.

If you notice a conference when you are online but decide against going to it, make sure, again, that you save the page to your favourites. 'Conference proceedings' is the term given to an account of a conference: effectively, some details about the event itself, some background on its instigation and a transcript of the papers given at the event. There might also be descriptive material or synopses of poster contributions or panel discussions. For some conferences, where papers have been distributed prior to the event, the proceedings may be released before the conference takes place. In some cases, only a selection of papers will be included and these might be subject to peer review and perhaps editing.

These were, at one time, produced in hard copy and circulated or sold to those scholars with an interest in the field. Nowadays they might be made available free, and far more quickly, online. By keeping track of conferences online you can become part of the dissemination world virtually before you take the plunge in person.

Through your institution/organisation: Making full use of the resources available in your organisation can mean more than just asking colleagues about events, or checking notice-boards. Training in presentation skills, or practice sessions as you prepare for an event, might be available, and you may find such events useful as a means of increasing your 'conference contacts'. Your organisation's intranet can be a useful means of gleaning information about events, both internal and external. You might also want to tap into the practical resources available to you, such as a 'travel fund' for conferences, if one exists in your organisation, and online bulletin boards which are useful for arranging lift shares and such like.

In offering you this list of options I have suggested that you 'stay in the loop' because I would urge you to employ all of these methods as early as possible, even before you have formed a clear idea about your ideal presentation topic or, perhaps, even committed absolutely to the idea of presenting your research. By getting an idea of what is happening on the conference circuit as early as you can you are putting yourself in a good position to gauge current areas of interest, to get a good sense of the conference formats that tend to work in your area, and to learn about research groupings which might give rise to future conferences. By the time you respond to a call for papers you will feel comfortable with the system and ready to be involved more actively.

By covering all bases in this way, you might by now be thinking that it is a lot of hard work, even at this early stage, but this need not be the case. Just dedicating a morning to carrying out some research into these sources of information will give you a good sense of where to go next, and it will also challenge you to think about how you need to proceed. Would a conference paper or presentation be right for you straight away, or would you rather attend a couple of conferences first, to get a feel for such events? Would a colloquium, a symposium or a research seminar be the type of start in dissemination that you would prefer? What type of dissemination event is most popular in your area of interest? Questions such as this, once answered, will give you a far more secure idea of where to go next.

I am going to finish this chapter with another question which might, by now, be lurking in the back of your mind, trying to push its way forward. What on earth have you achieved on which you could present? This question will become urgent the more you consider dissemination events and if it is left to move from a niggling query to a great big question mark it can sap your belief in your material.

I know that the chances are good that you already have material which could be worked up into an impressive presentation or conference paper. You knew this too when you picked up this book. Now that we have moved this far into considering dissemination, the reality might be becoming a little daunting and you could have lost confidence to such an extent that you cannot quite remember why you thought you were ready to move ahead and present.

 EXERCISE

We will be spending the rest of this book together, working through how you can best approach the challenge of presenting your material, so now is a good time for me to ambush you. If you were absolutely forced to do it, and I showed you no mercy at all, what three topics could you present on right now? Write them down here, going with your gut reaction, not giving yourself too much time to think:

1

2

3

What you will have written down are topic areas which are likely to be too broad for a conference paper, so now take each of the three and split them down:

1 A)

   B)

   C)

(Continued)

(Continued)

2 A)

B)

C)

3 A)

B)

C)

One of these could be your conference presentation. We will move on now, but when we come to examine the pool of material from which you might draw a conference paper or presentation, you could return here for inspiration. You might not use any of these topics, of course, but at least I hope that your confidence will now be higher: you *can* do this.

Four

PREPARING AN ABSTRACT/OUTLINE/ SYNOPSIS

What is an abstract/outline/synopsis?

When 'calls for papers' come out, potential speakers are usually asked to submit a proposal, which is effectively a sales pitch for their paper. Sometimes the term proposal is used, but the other terms used in the title of this chapter are equally common. Your own discipline might use one term or another as a preference, but the requirements relating to each are broadly similar.

 TOP TIP

If you are planning to give a group presentation, it is usually easiest for one person to produce an abstract, outline or synopsis, bringing together a vision which has been produced from the initial collaborative talks and plans. It is a good way to test whether you all share the same idea about the purpose and outline structure of the paper or presentation and, if you do, it is usually simple enough for other group members to make small amendments before it is submitted.

Your proposal might include some (but not necessarily all) of the following:

1. A word count element – usually, 300–500 would be a reasonable word count to expect for a conference call to papers. If there is no word count, it would still make sense to stick roughly to this length, following the old adage of 'leaving

them wanting more'. It is generally more productive to give a brief synopsis of your idea for a paper than to give a full version of what you intend, on the basis that you can develop a synopsis in the light of any discussions you have had with the organisers, rather than trying to remould a much longer document to suit.

2. Some biographical details, which might be no more than your title and position in an organisation, or might be a lengthier, narrative biography of your career and your research interests.

3. An outline of your proposed paper. Whatever you are asked to produce (abstract, outline or synopsis) the function of the document will be the same: to give a brief overview of what your paper or presentation will contain. Although etymologists and grammarians could happily argue for an afternoon about the precise meaning and function of the words, I will take them as synonymous in this context.

How will the call for papers help me to produce a proposal?

1. In the first instance make sure that the call for papers is actually referring to a conference. This sounds obvious, I know, but it is easy to get excited about a call for papers, especially an online call, only to find at the very end of the document that the papers in questions are actually for submission to a journal, not for presentation at a conference. It will still be an exciting thing to have found, but not quite what you were looking for.

2. Although you will be given the details of what to produce, look at the overall call before you commit to it. If, for example, it is hugely detailed, with rigid sections to the conference, with tightly defined themes, you could surmise that your proposal will only be successful if your area of research fits squarely into that niche. If the areas for exposition at the conference are broader, you may feel that you would like to submit a proposal even if your area of expertise is not quite a perfect fit.

3. The remit of the conference could be very wide. This would usually be indicated by a series of questions, designed to appeal to the curiosity of potential contributors, and a sense (or, often, an explicit statement) that papers around a central topic area are welcomed.

4. The call for papers should save you time, in two ways. The details you are offered should allow you to dismiss the idea of presenting at a conference, the name of which seemed perfect for you but the details of which have shown you that it is not the right forum for your work. Additionally, if you are uncertain you will now have contact details for the organisers. An email with a two-line outline of your idea for a paper, with a request as to whether a proposal might be of interest in this area, would save you having to work up a full proposal if the topic is not of interest to the organisers. However, only do this if the call for papers really does leave you in doubt; avoid emailing just for reassurance.

5. The structure of the conference is often outlined in a call for papers, and this could give you a good idea of which part of the conference would suit your

material best. A round-table event (or section of a larger event) might only be asking for perhaps 10–15 minutes of material, followed by a fairly open discussion; a panel discussion can be the same, but might also involve experts having submitted brief papers before the event and then sitting as a panel and simply answering questions at the conference. A stand-alone paper could be 30–40 minutes long, with perhaps a question and answer session following. However, if two or three papers are to be linked thematically and given in one conference session, you might be expected to reduce that to 20–25 minutes' worth of material. In some conferences there are workshops, for which you might be sharing your research and expertise but without giving a paper as such; instead you would be allowing delegates to work up their own ideas around your expertise. This can be an exciting challenge, but it takes a lot of confidence and considerable preparation, so make sure that you are ready for the challenge before you commit.

6. There is something rather more nebulous that you can sometimes glean from a call for papers – the level of control to be exerted (however politely) over the speakers. It might be useful for you to spend a little while working through a selection of online calls for papers so that you get used to the tone that is usually employed. You will then be in an excellent position to spot the call for papers which appears to have been written by a group of conference organisers who seem secretly to want to write and deliver every paper themselves. The parameters of the conference are laid out in detail, the topic areas for contributions are carefully worded so as to exclude the unconventional and the scope is so tightly drawn that there is little room for interpretation. I would not suggest that you avoid such events (this level of desire for control is often simply the nervous reaction of inexperienced organisers, who will relax as things progress) but I would urge you to be cautious and ready to defend your corner as to the shape and content of your contribution.

So what do I have to do to produce the proposal?

If I were to give you the simple instruction 'just write a brief outline of your paper' this would get you only so far. Instead, you will want to avoid problems before they arise, so here are some guidelines:

 CHECKLIST

1 **This is more than an outline of an idea:** it is an abstract/outline/synopsis/proposal for a paper. You will probably not have written the paper yet, so you are in a good position to be brief, but make sure that you give a sense in the outline of how your paper will be structured and how your argument will develop.

(Continued)

(Continued)

2 **Write from a plan, even a brief plan:** it could be dangerous to attempt a detailed plan at this stage, in case you need to make changes to your paper and would find it difficult if it is already planned meticulously, but working up a brief plan is the most effective way to achieve an impressive outline.

3 **Avoid exaggeration:** this is your sales pitch, and so you will want your outline to be bright and engaging, but avoid claiming that you can perform presentation miracles in the time you are allowed for the paper or presentation. Making an impact with a narrower focus is normally preferable to a loose, generalised presentation.

4 **There is no need to bamboozle anyone:** if English is not your first language, the introduction to this section will be a good example of what to avoid in your outline – 'bamboozle' is a very English idiom, suggesting a deliberately induced confusion, and it is not widely used. Remember that a variety of readers will consider your outline, not all of whom will be specialists in your area, so avoid subject-specific jargon and uncommon terminology whenever you can.

5 **Write your outline from a plan, not a paper:** if you already have a paper written, or you are planning to work up a paper from an already completed piece of writing, try to work back and make a retrospective plan of the piece, just listing the key points perhaps, and then write an outline from this rather than cutting and pasting sections of the original piece. Writing afresh from a plan is far more effective than trying to squash existing writing into an outline.

6 **Do exactly what you are asked to do by the organisers:** you will probably start out fully intending to do just this, but then temptation creeps in. Perhaps you should just offer them a little more material, or your full CV rather than the 'brief bio' for which they asked? Maybe they would like you to explain more fully why your research is unique, or share with them some reviewers' comments on your recent research? No. Just give them exactly what was requested and never any more or less.

7 **You could suggest a 'fit' for your paper:** having urged you to avoid adding additional material, this does not mean that you cannot make clear where you think your work might fit into the event schedule, so make sure you begin your outline with 'A panel paper covering …' or 'A 30-minute presentation on …', assuming that you feel your material is best served by one format or another. If you are happy to slant your material and contract or expand the content to fit different presentation formats, you could make this clear, too.

8 **Your outline could be dual purpose:** what you produce here might be used in the programme for the conference, especially if parallel sessions are run, so think of your final audience as well as the organisers.

9 **Never exceed the word count**: it is likely that your first draft of an outline will be too long, even though you have produced it from a plan and are trying to be brief. This is not necessarily a bad thing, as it gives you the chance to précis it and so consider which are the most important features of your paper or presentation. Even if you are busy and just want to get this task out of the way, make sure that you keep on with the work of reducing the word count until it is on target: organisers do not react well to potential presenters who ignore even the most basic of instructions.

10 **Remain outward facing – give them what they need:** for some presenters this is, perhaps, the most difficult part of producing an outline. The planning is productive, the précis can be fun, but remaining focused on your readers can easily be overlooked. A paper could be brilliant, but if the outline for it is obscure, or difficult to read, or concerned more with the writer than the reader, it may never see the light of day. At every stage think of the impact your outline will make: it needs to be well structured, clear and written in accessible language. If you are not completely confident, give it to a friend or colleague and ask them to describe the paper as they imagine it from your outline: this can be a revealing moment, and will either make you smile with relief or rush back to your computer for a rewrite.

Having finished this list of suggestions with the single most important aspect of writing an outline, you might find an example useful. Below is the description which appears on the back cover of another book in this series, entitled *Teaching in Higher Education*:

This book is designed to walk you step-by-step through various teaching experiences. It includes advice, practical exercises, top tips and words of warning on:

- seminar presentations to your peers
- leading undergraduate seminars
- choosing material for teaching
- preparing teaching aids
- giving lectures
- dynamic learning environments
- handling assessment
- working in a teaching team
- mentoring.

This is a practical 'how-to' guide that is supported throughout by accessible explorations of how teaching can support your research. Written by lecturers who have taught for many years, the 'voice of experience' sections will support and encourage you in your move towards becoming a successful and confident educator.

Lucinda Becker, an award-winning Senior Lecturer in the Department of English Literature at the University of Reading, and University Teaching Fellow, has spent her career committed to enhancing the skills and knowledge of undergraduates and research postgraduates, writing numerous successful study guides in the process.

Pam Denicolo has dedicated her working life, mainly at the Universities of Reading and Surrey but also providing support to many other institutions worldwide, to improving the training of and support for early career researchers and their supervisors, through research, teaching, writing and serving through membership of influential national and international committees.

There are some techniques of effective précis which you might want to note from this example of an outline:

- No words are wasted on describing the basics of what the book is about – we assume that the reader can grasp this from the book's title. Work on your conference paper title in a similar way so that you can reduce the basic descriptive material to a minimum.
- From the outset, the focus is on what the reader will gain from reading the book. Organisers need to choose your paper, but your potential audience might also need to know why your paper is the one to choose.
- A sense of the structure of the book is given in the opening section – this would equate to you suggesting in your outline whether you see the material as a full presentation or a briefer paper, perhaps for a panel discussion.
- Bullet points are used to give the briefest possible outline of the content. You might or might not want to use bullet points, depending on your style of writing, but you could use them in the early stages of preparing your outline, so as to force you to be brief and to the point.
- The brevity of the bullet-pointed section, giving content detail, has allowed space for further consideration of the reader's experience in the final section of the outline. It is intended to be engaging and reassuring. You might intend to be challenging and controversial, or intriguing and contentious, but the principle remains the same: giving a flavour of the experience you hope to create.
- The brief biographies were, inevitably, the most difficult section to write in this description. Between us, the two authors have more than 50 years' experience of teaching, so when we wrote these bios we had the agonising task of leaving out much of the detail of our professional lives and focusing only on those aspects of ourselves which would be of interest, we hope, to those who are deciding whether or not to buy the book.
- As I have suggested for you, we also had an expert 'critical friend' to hand as this description was produced: the publisher would not have accepted anything that did not work well in this context.

Your conference abstract/outline/synopsis/proposal is not, of course, a book description, but you might like to return to this example as you produce it to make sure that you have achieved each of these objectives.

Five

CONFERENCE PAPER OR PRESENTATION?

The level of engagement with the material required of a conference presenter can vary hugely from one event to another. You may have noticed that I have been referring in this guide to your 'paper or presentation', and this is because either of these might be required of you. 'Giving a paper' once meant just that: an academic sitting down in a room with an audience listening as the paper was read aloud. No eye contact was required and no questions or other interventions would be expected until silence fell at the end of the paper reading. I have suggested here that this was the way things were done in the past, but this could still be the case if, for example, you were being asked to give a paper at a research seminar or symposium. However, 'giving a paper' could also, nowadays, mean giving a full-scale presentation, with data projector, handouts and several breaks for comments and questions.

The terminology is no friend to a presenter here. In the same way that being invited to 'give a paper' is no guarantee that you are simply going to be reading your work aloud to others, neither does being asked to 'contribute a presentation' ensure that the organisers are expecting a full-scale presentation. There are also, naturally, some events where both forms of dissemination (and anything in between) are acceptable, but you do need to know in advance what might be expected of you.

To some extent the differences between dissemination methods are related to subject or discipline areas, so you might be able to ask around, or attend a few conferences, so as to get a good feel of what is considered to be the norm in your field. There is no easy way to ascertain from a call for papers or other advance publicity what type of presentation is expected, so I would always advise that you check as soon as your paper is accepted. I would not especially urge you to find out before you submit your proposal, because the form need not have any impact upon your decision to submit an outline, but as soon as it has been accepted and you start to prepare, make sure that you are absolutely clear about what is expected of you.

During the course of your career you are likely to be sharing your ideas in a variety of ways, so it might be useful here to consider the advantages and disadvantages of different methods:

Giving a paper

How does it work?

- You sit or stand and simply read your paper to an audience, after which members of the audience might ask questions.
- Your paper might be circulated in advance.

What are the advantages?

- You have a high level of control over the event because you know exactly what you are going to say.
- Your audience might feel more relaxed, knowing that you have the paper right there in front of you and so are unlikely to make any blunders.
- You do not have to worry about technology, or moving around.

What are the disadvantages?

- It can be difficult to remain vibrant and engaging if you are struggling to maintain eye contact as you read.
- If the paper has been circulated in advance there is the danger of the audience becoming bored.
- Reading aloud can result in a tendency to speak in a monotone and speed up, so it takes practice.

 TOP TIPS

- Try to avoid too many rehearsals, as this can lead to a monotonous presentation style.
- Intersperse your paper with notes such as 'expand here' or 'add detail here' so that you can go off script for just a few moments so as to enliven the event, but only do this once you feel confident about your ability to give a paper.

- Notes such as 'smile', 'talk slowly', 'eye contact' and 'halfway' can help to keep you on track and keep your audience engaged.
- When you rehearse the paper, listen out for 'written English' as opposed to 'spoken English' as this can grate a little with the audience. Think, for example, about how many times you would use words and phrases such as 'furthermore', 'prohibitively', 'proceed' and 'finally, in conclusion' in your everyday speech. These need to be amended in your paper as much as possible.
- If your paper is being circulated before the event, take out the 'notes to self' you have included in your 'script paper', and also think about handouts. Using a handout, where you can go off script and ad lib for a while, can help to break up the event and enliven it, without throwing you off course too much.

Giving a full-scale presentation

How does it work?

- You may still read, this time from a script, but you are more likely to be working from prompt cards or, if you are confident in your ability to do so, from the natural prompting of the data projection screen.
- You will be standing with nothing (except perhaps a lectern) between you and the audience, each member of which will expect good eye contact, plenty of facial expression and a confident stance.
- You will expect questions and comments from audience members, either at the end of your presentation or at the end of a group of presentations.

What are the advantages?

- You have more choices about how you present your material and so can, potentially, create a more exciting event for your audience.
- You might be able to fit more material into the time available.
- You can involve your audience more in the event, should this suit your purposes.
- You can make more of an impact on your audience as a person, so it can be useful for networking.

What are the disadvantages?

- It takes more confidence to get it right, but this will come with practice.
- More can go wrong, so you need back-up plans in place.
- The likely response of a more excited audience is less easy to predict.

TOP TIPS

- Be clear about when you expect audience intervention. Audience members need to know whether you are happy to be interrupted as you go (unlikely, in most cases) or whether you expect comments or questions at the end.
- It is a good idea to let people know how long you expect your presentation to last, and how long they will be given to ask questions or make comments.
- Always, always have a back-up for the presentation aids you are using. Data projectors can fail, demonstrates can fall apart and even the humble overhead projector relies on a working bulb.

Giving an interactive presentation

How does it work?

- You are still giving a presentation, but you are asking the audience to respond throughout the event, rather than just at the end.
- The audience involvement might take the form of a survey or poll, or short breakout groups. It might involve online polling with results immediately available, or regular question and answer sessions throughout the presentation.

What are the advantages?

- Audience members feel part of a process; their views are being canvassed and their responses really matter to you.
- There is less intense, unwavering focus on you standing up and delivering.

What are the disadvantages?

- You need to be ready to change some of your choice of material for presentation in response to the audience interaction – this can be challenging.
- Potentially, you need to be able to present some material without a script, as you will be responding directly to audience members rather than having prepared in advance – this takes confidence in both the robustness of your material and in your ability to present.
- Audience interaction such as this frequently involves technology (smartboards with 'clickers', Twitter feeds, online polling through texting and so forth) and this does not always oblige at the crucial moment.

TOP TIPS

- If you are using 'instant technology' such as a Twitter feed or online polling responses which are sent direct to a screen behind you, try to arrange to have a supporter present to act as a monitor, filtering the responses for you before they hit the screen, just in case any rogue responses creep into the system.
- If you are going to include a group activity, make sure that there is space enough, without everyone having to start moving furniture.
- If you can, ask selected delegates in advance if they would be happy to be 'group leader' for one of the groups, urging them to ensure that feedback is timely and constructive.

Chairing a conference session

How does it work?

- You will introduce a speaker or set of speakers, listen to their papers or presentations and then 'field' questions. That is, questions from the audience will be addressed to you and you will either ask one speaker to respond, if there is only one speaker, simply nod encouragingly to the speaker when the first question is asked, inviting a response.
- If no questions are forthcoming, it would be up to you to ask the first question so as to get things moving.

What are the advantages?

- You need do no more than this, but you do get the benefit of conference delegates seeing your face as part of the conference; this is useful for networking.

What are the disadvantages?

- You do not get any opportunity to advance your own research position. You might introduce yourself very briefly before you introduce the speaker, but beyond this there is little to do.
- If the speaker is less than inspiring, you might have to think of several questions to ask. If the speaker has been contentious, you will have to referee between disagreeing experts.

TOP TIPS

- Your introductory remarks should be hugely complimentary – speakers rely on those chairing their session to boost their confidence at the last minute.
- However well you research a speaker, you cannot do as good a job as could the speaker, so ask the speaker or speakers to send you a little biography in advance, if time allows. That way you only say what pleases them and you will not be risking getting any detail wrong.
- Hold your nerve when it comes to questions. Often people take a little time to compose their thoughts, or to pluck up the nerve to ask a question, and they will not thank the chairperson who rushes in before them.

Presenting at a research seminar/colloquium/symposium/ research or interview panel

How does it work?

- This is a more low-key event, usually with a smaller audience, sometimes with no more than a dozen or so academics sitting around a room listening to a paper. It might involve a data projector or other presentation aids, but this would not necessarily be the case.
- Questions are usually confined to the end of the paper.
- Notice that I have included 'research or interview panels' in this category. Although the situation may be more nerve wracking in that you are hoping to have a research idea approved, or be awarded funding or offered a job, or given leave to progress to the next stage of your research, the principles are the same and so you could follow the advice offered throughout this guide as you approach these particular situations.

What are the advantages?

- This situation would usually be less demanding of your material than standing up in front of a large audience trying to give a full-scale presentation.
- You might be an invited speaker, in which case you could be fairly sure of an appreciative audience.

What are the disadvantages?

- These events are quite intimate affairs, so if you do get a difficult questioner it can be hard to diffuse the situation.
- You have to get your timing just right. If you talk for too long you will be depriving your peers of the chance to advance a position in relation to yours, and this can lead to frustration.

TOP TIPS

- Because these are often smaller events you need to make sure that you get all of the details right: Exactly how long will it last? What equipment, if any, will be available? How long should you leave for questions and discussion?
- There is sometimes a social element to research events such as this, so plan your timing so that you can stay on for a chat or a meal afterwards.

Leading a panel/round-table discussion

How does it work?

- You may or may not be giving a paper; your role is to ensure that the discussion which follows from any paper given runs smoothly.
- Discussion might be the only activity of the panel or round-table. The organisers may have circulated papers in advance ready for a discussion, or you might simply focus on possible answers to one research question in a discussion, rather than any formal papers being included.
- You will be expected to introduce your fellow speakers, ensure a smooth flow of Q & A and discussion, and close down the discussion in a timely way at the conclusion of the event.

What are the advantages?

- If this is an area of especial interest to you, you might enjoy taking charge of how the discussion develops.
- It might allow you to be involved in a conference and to share your research without having to prepare any presentation material in advance.

What are the disadvantages?

- You will be sharing the time with others, so you might not have sufficient chance to explore your specific research area with other interested scholars.
- If you struggle to keep control of meetings and such like, then you might have to concentrate on the practical elements of the event, to the detriment of your research dissemination.

 TOP TIPS

- If you know that you find chairing a meeting stressful, and you struggle to keep things to time, think twice about this: being a member of the panel might be better than leading it.

(Continued)

(Continued)

- Prepare as if you were introducing a presenter at a conference: ask the other speakers to send you the details that you could use to introduce them, if time allows.
- This is a shared event, so find out about the research activity of your fellow speakers, enough so that you do not just speak over them throughout, but rather dovetail their research activity to yours. This is an art, so do not expect this to go perfectly every time.

Contributing to a panel/round-table discussion

How does it work?

- The activity is as already described above, but your role is simply to contribute.

What are the advantages?

- There is less pressure on you and you can gain the benefit of listening to the views of others in closely allied areas of research rather than focusing solely on disseminating your own research.

What are the disadvantages?

- You have less time to make your point and you might risk being overlooked if the panel is made up of vociferous academics.

 TOP TIPS

- Discussions begun at a round-table or panel event often spill over into the next break in the conference programme; it helps if you can choose, in advance, the two or three points that you are determined to make so as to facilitate later discussion.
- Beyond making those points, relax and enjoy listening to your fellow scholars.

Running a conference workshop

How does it work?

- This is nothing like giving a paper. Instead, you will be leading a group of your peers through activities designed to elicit responses to your research.
- You might begin with a brief overview of both your work and the workshop set up, but after that the session will be activity based.

- Rarely, you might be giving a conference workshop which is based upon your research, but is designed to improve the skills set of the participants, rather than being principally concerned with the dissemination of your research.

What are the advantages?

- If prepared properly these are enjoyable and satisfying events to run.
- You will raise your profile within the academic community.
- The network of enthusiastic followers of your research will increase.

What are the disadvantages?

- Workshops take a fair amount of time to prepare and are only for the determined and the confident.
- There is often preparation work to do on the day itself, so you might miss seeing papers or presentations which are of interest to you.

 TOP TIPS

- Control your material; control your time; control your workshop participants. If you have doubts about your ability to do any of these things, think again about committing to this enterprise.
- Attending a few workshops should give you a good sense of whether you would be able to lead one in the future.

Knowing that there are so many ways in which you can contribute to an event will, I hope, inspire you to continue with your search for the perfect place to showcase your work. Of course, locating the event is just one stage; finding the material is the next challenge.

Six

CHOOSING MATERIAL FOR AN EVENT

The last section of the previous chapter will have given you a sense of the options open to you when you choose to disseminate your research, and you will be aware by now that each of these types of event or activity will make different demands upon you, but there are some constants around dissemination which I hope to share with you in this chapter. Until now this guide has been about the different forms of dissemination and an overview of how the system works; now we will face the first stage in the process of becoming an active participant: choosing material to present. I have based the structure of this chapter on the six most commonly asked questions I receive about this aspect of dissemination, so you can either read it straight through or skip first to the question which is of most interest to you right at the moment. Before I offer some detailed answers, here is the list of questions:

1. What shape will my paper be; how will my presentation look?
2. What should I avoid?
3. How much material will I need?
4. What sort of material would be suitable?
5. Where do I go to find material?
6. What about reusing previously disseminated material?

Now for the detail, with some checklists to keep you on track.

What shape will a paper be; how will my presentation look?

One of the easiest ways to picture a research paper or presentation is to think of it as a 'research sandwich'. You place down a piece of bread, which is the background to the research you are about to consider, then you add the filling, which is the research material itself, then you add the top slice of bread, which consists of your conclusions and/or your next set of research questions and/or areas for discussion. If the bread is plain white sliced bread, you are offering a simple explanation of how you came to your research and you will finish with just one of these options. If your bread is wholemeal multigrain, your opening might be a little more complex and you might choose to include more than one of the closing options.

As you may imagine, the sandwich analogy can be taken to all sorts of interesting places (I once heard an academic referring to a 'ciabatta roll of a presentation') but it has served its initial purpose here if it gets across the point that you need all three of these elements, in this order, if you are to give a satisfying presentation.

To stick with our sandwich for a moment, you need to think about the 'texture' of each element of your sandwich/paper/presentation. Your initial slice of bread must be thin and clearly sliced. An audience want to be reassured that an approachable human being is talking to them, so the opening section of your presentation might include a moment's personal digression – an anecdote to explain why you became so fascinated with your research area, for example. An explanation of how your work developed also helps to contextualise the research, but keep this clear and brief. The delegates need to know how you got here, but they are naturally most interested in the research itself. It can be useful to end this section of your paper or presentation with a clear set of research questions to which you have been trying to find answers. You will only be focusing on two or three of these, most usually, and some of the best presentations I have seen have relied solely on one precise and intriguing research question.

The clear slicing of that first piece of bread means that an audience will know when you are moving on to the 'filling of the sandwich'. You might move to a new slide at this point, or ask a rhetorical question (so, how did I go about finding a solution to this problem?).

  TOP TIP

A quick word here about rhetorical questions: they can really help to grip the audience's attention but limit their use to no more than one or two per presentation; they rapidly become irritating.

However you choose to do it, you need to ensure that the whole room is taking a mental breath with you before moving on to the filling. Of course, the filling is probably the part upon which you have been focusing up until now in reading this guide; it is difficult to remember that an audience needs the bread of the sandwich, however keen you are to share your ideas. When you are thinking about the filling you will need to consider how much of it is taken up with methodological explanation, how much with results and hard data and how much with your hypotheses, your interim conclusions and your musings. Learning how to prepare the filling so as to create the best impact will be the work of much of this guide.

The final slice of bread, as I have already suggested, need be far less thin and firm than your initial slice of introductory material. To decide how to shape this you will need first to consider your audience and its needs. It is relatively rare not to include any final conclusions; an audience needs to feel secure, to some extent, before feeling happy about asking you questions. If you feel that you cannot honestly draw any conclusions, and you are still convinced that, despite this, you have chosen the right material for the event, then you need to make clear to the audience why you are not able to offer the certainty of any conclusions at this stage of your research.

Sharing with the audience, through the top slice of bread, your next set of research questions can be an effective way to show the possible scope of your future activities, and can inspire an audience, but a word of caution is needed here. You might feel some anxiety about sharing too many of your great research ideas in such an open forum. If they are very unformed you risk looking foolish if an audience member can demonstrate that they are, for example, incompatible with your current research path. If an audience member is already carrying out research into one of the areas about which you have just speculated, you could be causing unnecessary resistance to your work. If you throw out several brilliant ideas for future research, it is possible that this might lead someone in a similar area to get around to exploring these areas before you get the chance to carry out the research. This would be perfectly acceptable, and you might be credited with having shared the research activity idea in the first place, but you would probably find it rather frustrating. So, if you are going to share some research questions which have arisen in your mind, take all of these possibilities into account as you vet each research question before you share it.

Suggesting areas for discussion to top off your sandwich can be a productive move in this situation. Whilst of course you cannot guarantee that the audience will only want to discuss the topics you have suggested (and an audience hates to feel that it is being led too firmly) it is likely that someone will pick up at least one of your suggestions. Try not to be too directive here, though. The question and answer or discussion session is the audience's time to be in control, to some extent, so ending your paper with 'so I thought that we might want to consider in the next few minutes …' is unlikely to gain you support.

   CHECKLIST

As you work through material for a paper, ask yourself about each stage of the 'research sandwich':

- Is my opening clear in terms of what I hope to achieve in this paper?
- Have I shared with the audience why this material is of interest to me?
- Have I been clear about my initial research questions?
- Is the main section of the presentation clearly divided between describing my research activities, considering the results of those activities and suggesting hypotheses?
- In the final section of my paper (the top slice of bread) is it clear which of the three options (conclusions, research questions, areas for discussion) I am including?
- If I am including more than one of these, will the audience know this and know which is which?

What should I avoid?

Naturally, you will make sure that every aspect of your research activity is ethically sound and has had, where necessary, approval from the appropriate ethics committee. None of your fellow scholars would seriously doubt this, given time to consider it, but if you introduce material which could in any way be construed as ethically problematic, this might cause problems. This is not because of your work as a researcher, but rather the nature of the occasion. Material mentioned in passing during a conference paper or presentation (or, even more problematic, during answers to questions) can leave an audience feeling uncomfortable. Did you really mean to include the material? Are you aware of the ethical implications of this turn in your research? If you mentioned it inadvertently, should they let you know that you have breached ethical conventions?

As you can see, ethics can cause you problems not of substance, but of reception. The last thing you need when you are disseminating your research is for some members of the audience to be looking at you anx-iously or to seem uncomfortable asking questions or engaging in discussion about your findings. Clear this up at the outset: if there is any chance at all that ethically approved material will be included in the talk itself, or in your response to questions or discussions afterwards, reassure your audience as you begin that you have clearance to disseminate publically all of the mate-rial you are including.

Unproven material is equally likely to make an audience anxious, and yet there are occasions when you might wish to include some findings which are speculative and which you half expect might be refined or rejected upon further analysis. You might, for example, want to share with delegates your excitement at a possible new line of inquiry, aware that it is only days since you first stumbled across what seems, at first glance, to be robust material. There is no need to shy away from the inclusion of unproven material but, as with the situation surrounding ethics, just make sure that every audience member is clear about the level of claim you are making for any material you choose to include in your paper or presentation.

There are two research positions you might take which should not be avoided, but need to be handled well: conventional and contentious. These are, of course, diametrically opposed positions, and each throws up its own set of problems. We are all, as the saying goes, standing on the shoulders of giants. Each new piece of research will necessarily, to a greater or lesser extent, be based upon the earlier work of others. The secret to a good presentation is to acknowledge the giants upon whom you are relying, and to contextualise your research within a conventional, accepted knowledge base, but then to move on firmly to your own activities. This is not necessarily easy to do in the early stages of your presenting career: the conventional is such a deliciously safe place to be. Moving on takes courage, but you need to do it so that you can showcase your own, unique contribution to knowledge.

Contentious material sounds perfect for a conference. Indeed, it sometimes seems as if conferences are simply full of academics arguing over contentious issues for hours on end. In reality, this is not the case. Contentious material does, without doubt, form part of the excitement of a conference: one expects to be intrigued and to have one's views challenged by others in a similar field of expertise. However, contentious material is most usually offered as the very tip of the iceberg of a paper – perhaps in the closing moments when new research questions are postulated, or as one section of an otherwise interesting but uncontentious exposition of research. This is not to say that papers which offer a wholly contentious viewpoint are never presented, they are, and they can be masterful and inspiring, but you would need to be ready for the intense scholarly scrutiny which would follow such a paper.

 TOP TIP

Balance the level of convention and contention in any paper you give – asking your supervisor, mentor or critical friend to consider just this aspect of a paper you are planning will help ensure that the response you get is the one you expect.

There is one type of paper/presentation which is not simply potentially problematic, but rather must be avoided at all costs: the unfocused ramble or rant. These occur occasionally, either when a scholar has not had time or material enough to prepare (the ramble) or when a researcher feels under undue pressure to defend a position so that judgement becomes muddled (the rant). The simple rule to follow is this: if you are not crystal clear about what you want to say in a paper or presentation, and why you want to say it, say nothing.

What sort of material would be suitable?

Before you begin on the process of planning and preparing your paper or presentation, you will want to take a step back and consider the type of material which would best suit the occasion. For this, you need to consider your audience and the practical variables of the day, but first you need to think about your principal purpose in giving a paper or presentation: why do you want to give this particular paper?

 CHECKLIST

There are several commonplace answers to this question and a checklist will help you focus on what is driving you:

- to find answers to some research questions which bother me;
- to gain clarity in an area;
- to glean some new ideas for the next stage of my research project;
- to test my existing ideas for moving forwards;
- to gauge the response to my next publication;
- to mine the expertise around me for the next stage of my research;
- to network professionally and intellectually;
- to disseminate my research.

You can see that each of these motivators will have an impact upon your paper, both in terms of structure and content, so you might wish to return to this checklist later as we work through the planning and preparation stages.

Having thought about your position as a starting point, you will need to move swiftly to a consideration of the audience's position – the audience members are the most important factors in this equation. Think first about the level of expertise in the room: a talk to your local history society would necessarily require a greater level of explanation about your own, very niche area of interest than would a specialised presentation to the 'Huguenot Society of Great Britain and Ireland'. If the case is less clear cut, do not feel awkward about contacting the organisers to make some enquiries about the expected audience members. This is far better than appearing with inappropriately pitched material.

Although it is not always possible to do this, research being a complicated process, it can help sometimes to think of your paper or presentation in terms of 'takeaway points'. In a talk of any length you will be focusing on getting across no more than six main points; you can expect each audience member to recall just two or three of these points the day after the event. Thinking in these terms, it becomes obvious that focus is going to be important; if you can identify your takeaway points, perhaps even putting them on a final slide through a data projector or on a handout, this can certainly increase the impact of your contribution to an event.

Mentioning slides brings me to the final point to consider in this section: the practicalities of the occasion. However unlikely it seems that there would be no data projector, make sure that it will actually be available to you if you choose to use this means of conveying part of your message. If it is available, then you might want to slant your presentation more towards impressive visual material unless, of course, every other speaker is likely to do the same and you want to arrest the attention of the audience by taking a different approach: more on this when we come to think about presentation aids.

In practical terms you might also like to think about the mechanics of the event. You could find out, for example, whether you will be given a choice about how much time is devoted to your paper or presentation and how much is to be given over to the question and answer session which arises from it. You might also have a choice about the time of day you are to give your paper, or even how long your paper should be. These practicalities are worth firming up before you begin to plan.

 TOP TIP

If you are thinking of presenting as part of a team, the practicalities need even more care, especially in the early stages. Make sure that you work together as a team right from the outset, keeping the lines of communication open at all points and giving each member the chance to contribute. If you are geographically diverse and so can only talk online, or if you are all incredibly busy, it can help to designate one member of the team as the chairperson or organiser. This person would not have any more say than anyone else in the content of the paper or presentation, but would ensure that the preparation was carried out in a timely way and that each team member kept to an agreed schedule.

How much material will I need?

To some extent this will be dictated by the choices you have already made about your audience's needs, your takeaway points, your use of visual aids and so forth, but there are guidelines you can follow.

If I were to give a lecture of about 50 minutes, with half a dozen places where I might improvise on a point for a minute or so, I would aim to write 4,000 to 5,000 words of continuous prose. Having checked with colleagues, this seems to be a reasonably standard amount of material to be included in a lecture. Although you are not giving a lecture as such, this rough word count could still apply if you are going to be disseminating information in a similar way, such as giving a paper – the odd pause for effect and a few points of ad lib but, other than those, fairly continuous prose.

If you are giving a presentation, rather than a paper, you will not be able to work with a word count because you will be presenting from prompt cards/notes or the prompt of your slides. If you have not had much presenting experience, it can be useful to produce a full script to the word count suggested here, time it for accuracy and then reduce your script to prompts; I will be covering this in more detail in the chapter on preparing to present.

Advising you as to the number of slides you might need to convey your material is a far more difficult thing to do. There are several points for you to consider. Think about presentations you have seen in your field – do you think that your discipline area tends to use plenty of slides to get the message across, or only a few? This is not, I know, relating the number of slides to your particular presentation, but audiences do tend to have expectations as to the number of slides they would generally expect to see. Using too few slides is rarely a problem, unless you ask your audience to look for too long at a used slide or a blank screen, but too many slides can make an audience feel rushed. Slides with too much information on them leave an audience feeling resentful because they cannot keep up. In general, my advice would be to completely ignore the issue of slides until quite late in the process.

In choosing your material, whether for a paper or a presentation, you will be deciding on key points to cover. Remember as you plan that your word count, timing and/or number of slides will be affected by the fact that you need to include a solid introduction and a persuasive conclusion; it is surprising how easy it is to forget this in the planning stages. Remember too the research sandwich. You will need to decide on the ratio of 'bread' to 'filling'. In some situations you will need a lengthy introduction and grounding to your research area, with relatively little new material or argument; at other events the introduction can be far briefer and more time will be dedicated to your research findings and hypotheses.

The time you give over to the 'top slice of bread' depends on what you plan to gain from the experience. If you are aiming simply to showcase well-established work then your 'top slice' might be no more than a brief résumé of what you have already said; if you are hoping that the audience will help you to tease out some knotty issues then it might be far longer, as you set the stage for a far more lengthy and discursive question and answer session. The difference between these two responses is not just chance: you can make it happen as you plan your talk and organise your material.

 TOP TIP

It is safe to assume that whatever topic you have in mind as you approach a paper or presentation will be too large – that is just human nature. Be prepared to cut it down, and down again, as you move through the process.

Where do I go to find material?

We have now reached the heart of the challenge facing you. It is all very well for me to be offering you advice on how much, and which type of, material to use, but where on earth are you to find any material at all, let alone the right material? The sense of simply not having material to present is very common. From my experience, it is certainly the reason I have been offered most frequently, far outstripping nerves, lack of experience or any practical difficulty. This is partly, I think, the result of a natural diffidence from which many experts suffer. We are so acutely conscious of those giants' shoulders upon which we stand that we often feel, quite wrongly, that what we have to say will not be erudite enough, innovative enough, good enough.

We can also suffer from a reluctance to come out of our 'research bub-ble'. The isolated nature of much research activity is often bemoaned, but it can also be a comfortable, indeed a charming, place to be. You can hypothesise as much as you like, you can scatter material around your intel-lectual playground with no need to clear it up and sort it out until you are ready, and you can allow your ideas and opinions to firm up at their own pace and largely of their own accord. A public airing of your work naturally disrupts all of that for a short while and it is only natural that this might feel uncomfortable, especially for a relatively new presenter.

Your reaction to this potential discomfort might, understandably, be to offer at a conference or other public event only that material which you are sure in your own mind is polished and complete material, in as much as any research material can ever be considered complete; if you are aiming simply to impress and network, this could be a fruitful approach. However I would urge you for a few minutes to consider the possibility of a different approach, with potentially different results. If what you want from the experience is feedback from your peers, a plethora of research avenues opening up to you, a scattering of new ideas for your research journey and advice from those with far more research experience than you, then perhaps it is worth being a little less rigid in what you present.

One way I like to think of this is to consider your research paper or presentation as a sponge-cake mix, which you put into the oven about 30 minutes ago. Your presentation or paper is like you turning on the light in the oven for all to see. The base and sides of the cake are cooked (your introduction and grounding in the topic are the base, your argument and established hypotheses are the sides), but the middle of the cake is still soft and damp, ready to rise and give the cake its final form. The question and answer session and any discussion which ensues is the heat which allows the rest of the cake to take shape: it will still be your cake, and will still turn out fairly much as you expect, but it might be just a little bit higher, a little bit nearer to perfect as a result of you sharing it with others.

The analogy of a cake might cut across your assumptions. You may have presumed that the best way to approach the occasion would be to offer a complete chapter of a thesis or a full-length article which you plan to publish. This would be a logical approach, but to offer your audience the completely cooked, indeed cooked and cooled, cake might be to miss an opportunity. The cake will, of course, look perfect but the only option your fellow scholars have is to admire it or take a slice out of it by querying an entire premise of your work. This need not be destructive, and it could give exciting grounds for debate, but it might not move your research forward significantly, and you would need to be ready for this outcome.

It can be easier, and more productive in terms of the occasion, to work up new material for a paper or presentation. This might be wholly new, worked up from some research ideas upon which you are working at the moment, or it might be relatively new. If you carry with you a research notebook or some such, in which you jot down ideas as they come to you, this would be a good time to read through what you have there in case an idea inspires you. Alternatively, if you would rather not work from scratch, an essay or report written at an earlier stage of your career could be reviewed now in the light of the paper ahead of you. Has it been superseded by later research, or might it be a fruitful area to return to for a while, working it up more fully and then testing the hypotheses on an audience of your peers? A planned or draft thesis or book chapter, or an essay contribution to a publication which you have been mulling over, might usefully be shared at a conference.

There are two advantages to this approach: you will gain support for current rather than past areas of intellectual endeavour and, generally speaking, it is easier to work up material from a low word count or from a plan than it is to cut down or refashion existing material. If you are aiming to rework fully-formed, existing material, it is a good idea to retrospectively plan it. That is, read through the piece with marker pen in hand, noting the key points and then listing them as if they were points on a plan. That way you can work up each point to make a persuasive conference argument, rather than presenting the material in the style of formal, written English, which has obviously been extracted from a longer piece.

 TOP TIP

There is an important exception to the suggestion that newer material tends to be better for conference papers and presentations than already formed material. If you have produced a chapter or journal article which is yet to be published and you would genuinely welcome feedback and suggestions on it from your peers, then this would work. That is, as long as you really are happy to have the piece critiqued. Make sure that you begin your paper or presentation by explaining that this is a draft publication to the audience members so that they know what you are hoping to gain from them.

What about reusing previously disseminated material?

There is not necessarily an embargo on reproducing previously disseminated material at a conference or other public event. After all, you would like to disseminate your material to the widest possible audience, and your fellow scholars would be happy to hear about it, but there are a few things to consider before taking this option:

 CHECKLIST

- Be absolutely clear about who possesses this intellectual property (IP). Did you sign over the copyright to another party? If you did not sign it over in its entirety, did you agree contractually to a restricted dissemination of the material away from its point of publication, in either hard copy or electronic form?
- Can you be sure that the vast majority of the audience members will not have heard the material before? If a few have, it is not a problem. Indeed, they may enjoy the chance to hear and ruminate on it again.

- If you are planning to rework the material, take a moment to consider whether it is fit for purpose. Some types of material work better as refashioned outputs than others. If you wrote the piece or talked to a web camera with reference to a very specific area of research for a niche audience, you will need to rework it and how well this can be achieved will need to be explored at this stage.
- Forget your audience for a moment: will the material bore you? This sounds simplistic, but if you have disseminated material in several forms over several years you might need to take a break from it so as to refresh your enthusiasm for sharing your research; disseminating a new area of your research could do this.

In this chapter our focus has been on how to choose material to present to others. In the next chapters I will be working with you on what to do with your chosen material as you work it up into a paper or presentation. If, at any time, you start to have doubts about the material, how effective it will be or how suitable for your chosen audience, you might usefully return to this chapter to consider whether the problem is in your preparation or whether it is more fundamental and requires you to return to the ingredients in your research and start on a new cake.

Seven

PREPARING YOUR MATERIAL

This chapter is all about planning: why to do it, how to do it and how to make the most of it. The very first thing we need to do is to establish whether you are a natural planner or not. Think about next weekend: will you have a list of things to do? Think about your last food shopping trip: did you have a firm shopping list? Think about your dream holiday: would you know in advance what you wanted to see and do on most of the days, even before you got there? If you answer 'yes' to these questions then you probably are a natural-born planner. These may not be written lists of plans: extremely organised people can be writing lists and making logical plans in their head all the time and so can seem quite casual, but they are mentally planning all the time.

There is no inherent advantage to being either a natural planner or non-planner in most activities. Planners, if given a task, will carry it out efficiently and often at some speed, whilst non-planners are more likely to take more time as they dally along the way. Non-planners may put off deadlines, but the planner is more likely, when carried away with enthusiasm for completion, to leave out one important element of a project and would then have to go back and refine the outcome. These natural tendencies also apply to life as a researcher. The planner may have an entire thesis planned in the first few months of a doctoral programme, but will then have to go through the painful process of picking apart and restructuring the plan as a result of research. The non-planner will be happier to let the plan grow with the research, but might suffer the stress of never feeling that things are quite under control.

 TOP TIP

Your personality type in this regard can also come into play if you are planning a group presentation. Planners can sometimes be so rigid in their approach to a plan that they simply cannot see that any other way but theirs could work and get the message across. Non-planners can be easier to work with in one way – they could be more open to ideas – but they might drive others to distraction with their refusal to pin down their ideas into a presentation format.

I would argue that you can spot an unplanned presentation without any hesitation. Please avoid being taken in by those scholars who proudly announce to anyone who will listen that they never do more than scribble down a few ideas on the back of an old envelope and are then equipped to give an inspirational, hour-long presentation. Still less should you believe those who claim not to bother with any notes at all, preferring to extemporise on the whim of a scholarly moment. Planning ensures that you give the best possible view of your research, that you highlight only the most salient features of a project, that you stay in command of the occasion throughout and that you do it with an inner confidence that is difficult to derive from anything less than punctilious planning.

Having spent a few moments being asked to think about planning, your response is already likely to be dictated by whether or not you are a natural planner. If you are not, you might already be wondering if you could skip parts of this chapter, but I hope that the novelty of considering planning in this context might keep you reading through until the end. If you are a natural planner, you will probably enjoy the chapter, as it will confirm much of your usual approach to tasks, but you might then go away and develop further the ideas suggested here, so that you create your own, customised system of planning. If you are an extreme natural planner you might find some of the suggestions overly laborious and might even be irritated at times during the chapter, because your instinct will be to do no more than put down a few headings and bullet points and expand straight to a paper or presentation from there. Try to stick with it, whichever type of person you are, so that you at least know about the options open to you when it comes to planning your next presentation.

You might use the planning methods suggested here in one of two ways: either to plan from scratch, or to take apart an existing piece of writing so as to refashion it ready for a presentation; I will be explaining the process from both angles. If you are not used to planning, you might like to plan something from scratch first, just to get into the swing of how to plan, before you set yourself the task of retrospective planning, which can be a little more challenging.

Your six-point plan

The first thing you will need to do is to make, as fast and instinctively as you can, a list of the key points you feel you *need t*o cover in your presentation.

This will be a list of no more than six points; for most presentations, it would be only three or four points. When I say here the points you need to consider, 'need' is the crucial word. Making a six-point plan is not easy. If you give yourself too long to think about it, you will naturally digress into many more points as they occur to you, points which you would like to make because they are impressive, or fascinating, or witty. However, this would lead you astray into having a dozen or more main points and the purpose of the exercise is lost.

If you are doubting for a moment that human beings really are only happy with six main points for their consideration, think about how many main headlines are offered in a daily news broadcast. The show may last for 20 or 30 minutes, but the headlines will only cover four to six of the stories which will be told. Think also of keynote political speeches: they may have huge depth and range overall, but the speaker knows that only five to six main points will be reported in the press, because we do not want to remember more than that. On a more mundane level, think about washing machines. It matters not a bit that they are becoming increasingly complex, with many different functions to choose from: it is unlikely that you would use more than six of the options being offered to you.

The most effective way to establish your six (or three, four or five) main points is to force yourself to jot them down at speed. You need to feel pressured if you are to be able to focus only on the most important points, so write down the topic area for your presentation (as it stands now, aware that you might narrow it down or nuance it later) and give yourself just one minute to write down the main points you would want to convey to an audience. If you are retrospectively planning from an existing document, take a highlighter pen and force yourself to read it through at some speed, putting a highlighted number in the margin whenever you get to a main point. Do this on a spare copy of the document first, with back-up copies ready, so that if you find yourself having marked up 17 main points, you can try again. If you really cannot reduce the document down to six points, you need to consider whether it is susceptible to being reworked into an effective presentation.

The purpose of creating a six-point plan is twofold: it forces you to look at the 'bigger picture' of what you are trying to convey, and it gives you a possible outline for your presentation. (I say here a 'possible' outline because it may be that, later in the process, you discard some of these points, or adapt them in some way.) You now need to put aside your six points. During the next part of the process you may want to glance at them occasionally for inspiration, but no more than that. If you slavishly try to follow them as you make a more detailed plan you are likely to miss opportunities to create the best possible plan. We will return to them later as a sort of insurance policy for your presentation, but now we will consider together how to move on to the next stage.

Your detailed plan

There are as many methods of planning as there are people to do the planning. As a new method is designed, somebody will refine it and redesign parts of it such that, over time, it can be claimed as a new method. You may already be familiar with several planning methods, and each has something to recommend it. Here I will be using just one method, the spider chart, and there are several reasons for this. The first is that the spider chart seems to suit the way most people tend to think. It is rare for someone to find that the method is not conducive to their natural way of thinking, so it is a fairly safe bet in this guide. The second is that it lends itself rather well to presentations. This is because you are usually, in a presentation, aiming to share with an audience a diversity of information which has been fitted together in such a way that it suits your purpose for just that occasion. Often you are creating an argument, which works very well with a spider chart, but even if you are principally trying to show a process (for which a flow chart might seem like the most natural method of planning), you will still be framing it with introductory and concluding material, and perhaps some steers towards the end as to the discussion areas and the questions you would welcome.

The final reason I have for using spider charts in this context is that they are easy to create and they are very human in their creation. That is, we tend to use pens on paper to create them rather than computer programs. Some scholars enjoy using coloured pens or pencils to create them, and this is all to the good. Although some people find planning software useful, in my experience most of us work best with pen on paper. This ensures that your plan remains human in scale: eight pages of printed out computerised plan that you stick on a wall can be daunting rather than informative. It is, usually, easier to throw the plan away and start again if it is just a rough plan on a piece of paper; it is also easier for most people to cross through one section of a hand-drawn plan if they decide to discard it. I notice that Prezi®, an increasingly popular piece of presentation software, often looks a little like a glorified spider chart, so it allows presenters to use an intuitive form of planning and seamlessly develop it into a full-blown presentation in one movement.

We will work through the creation of a spider chart together here, so I can consider with you the important aspects of each stage. A spider chart begins life with just one circle in the centre of a piece of paper. The words you put in that circle are crucial: they must be few in number and should encapsulate the essence of your presentation. For the purposes of this example I am going to assume that the presentation we are planning together is, in keeping with my earlier analogy, entitled 'The art of making a stupendous birthday cake for a five-year-old little girl'. This presentation, although simple (and, I must admit, fairly unlikely!) and not research related, will serve to illustrate the points I want to make whilst being accessible to all.

My six-point plan, which is based on my gut reaction to this topic, would look like this:

- flavour;
- shape;
- fillings;
- height;
- decorations?;
- cost.

I will put this list to one side for now, but glance at it if I feel that I am getting lost and need a reminder of where I started. As I begin work on my spider chart, the sheet of paper will look like this:

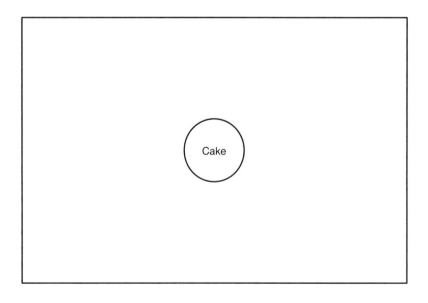

Note that the whole title is not there: just the essential words (or word, in this case) which will give you an instant outline of your primary purpose. With every presentation plan, regardless of topic area or overall purpose, I would then add two of the 'feet' of the spider:

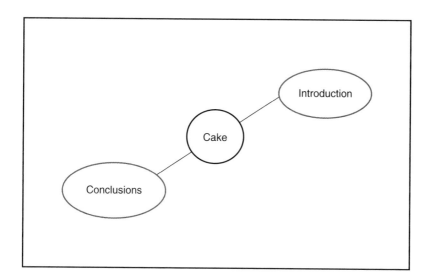

Where you put your 'introduction' and 'conclusions' feet will probably be instinctive. Illogically, this is where I tend to place mine, rather than side by side. I think this is because I find that breaking up the order of the other feet of the spider with these standard feet (as you will see in a moment) helps me to remain flexible in my approach and more prepared to change my mind and cross out or alter feet which are not really working. Now that I have two spider's feet I might want to complicate them a little. This might happen at the outset or additions might come to me as the plan progresses. That is one of the reassuring things about planning like this: every thought is captured as you go along, so that no detail is lost as you form the overall shape of the presentation. Let's assume that, at this early stage, I only have a couple of things to add to my first spider feet.

I am now clear that I will need to mention the basic facts at the outset – it is a cake for a little girl who is five. I have also realised that I might want to mention at the end that I must find out if she is vegetarian, and ask whether anyone in the audience has ever made a vegetarian cake, as this will have an impact on how I go forward after the event.

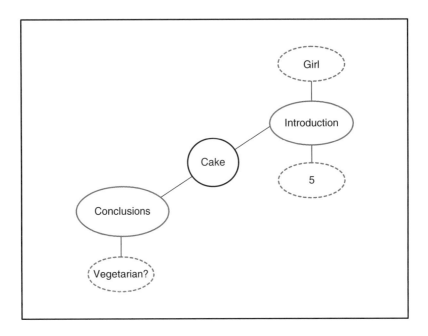

Now I need to add feet for the principal areas of my presentation. Remember that, however complex each of these might become, your audience will struggle with more than four to six main points:

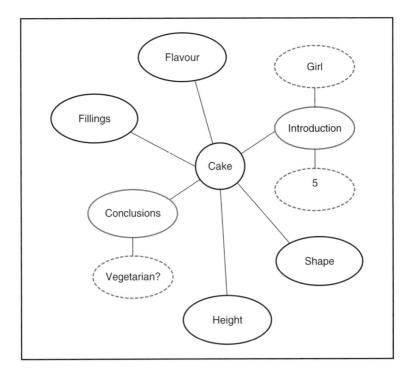

I have chosen to include four main areas for my presentation: flavour, fillings, shape and height. I can then expand each of these:

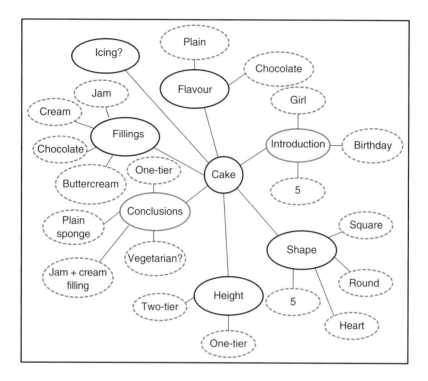

By now the spider chart is quite full, but it is not difficult to read. What is more, it is quite clear that some sections of my presentation will take longer than others (I have four filling options, for example, compared to only two flavour options to discuss). I realised that I had not mentioned anywhere that this is to be a birthday cake, so I have now included this in the introduction area of the plan. I also noticed that I had not considered whether the cake was to be iced or not. I would not have time in my presentation to give a significant amount of space to this, but I should mention it, so I have included it as one simple foot, with nothing leading off it, as simply a question to ask. At this stage it sits in the main body of the presentation; later I might decide to make it a subsection of the conclusions area, as a topic for discussion to raise with the audience at the end of the presentation.

I could make other changes at this stage, and this might relate to the fact that I would choose this moment to look back on my first six-point plan to see what had happened to it. This was my initial list:

- flavour;
- shape;

- fillings;
- height;
- decorations?;
- cost.

The first four of these are on my plan, the issue of decorations has been reduced to a single question about whether or not the cake should be iced, and, having remembered that the little girl in question is an adored relative, I have decided that the cost of the cake is irrelevant. My six points were not wrong; they just needed more consideration. You will find this with your first points too: the sign of a good planner is one who is prepared to change the plan as often as is necessary to make sure that it is right.

A mention here of organisational dyslexia might be useful. If you find that making a plan for a presentation is taking you far longer than you had expected because you keep changing your mind beyond what you think is useful, or if making plans leaves you feeling anxious and confused rather than organised and reassured, you might be suffering from a form of dyslexia which is keeping you from achieving your best through planning. This will not be an insurmountable problem and there are plenty of strategies for you to try so as to overcome this hurdle. If you think this might be a problem for you, getting help as early as you can will free up more of your time to make productive plans for impressive presentations.

For those people who are extreme natural planners, with highly logical brains and an innate sense of order, the problem might be quite the opposite. These scholars can sometimes suffer from a rigidity of thought which thwarts them as they try to plan. They find it difficult to change their mind once something is set down on paper, and might argue for the inclusion of each of their original points if they are working in a group situation, even if it is clear to everyone else that these points need more work or should be discarded. Although one might not expect it, this can be as unproductively time consuming as organisational dyslexia, because the rigid thinker will forge ahead, reluctant to change any of the points in the presentation, and might, as a result, produce a presentation which is missing some crucial elements. When, usually at the rehearsal stage, these omissions are discovered, it can take a significant amount of time to restructure the entire presentation so as to include them at such a late stage.

Thinking about the fact that different scholars react to planning in very different ways brings me, for a moment, to the emotional response you might have to planning. This might sound a little odd, but it is the case that, for most of us, planning is an emotional process. It can be intensely frustrating if the plan does not look right but you cannot work out what is wrong with it; equally, it can be hugely irritating if you are planning a group presentation and other members of the group agree to use a planning method with which you do not feel comfortable. The positive obverse to this is that when a plan runs smoothly and finally encapsulates perfectly what you want to cover in a presentation you will feel calmer, more in control and confident that you can say what you want to convey with conviction.

As an individual presenter you will be able to choose the planning method which suits you best, but even here there may be elements of the presentation process with which you feel less happy. For example, some presenters are very happy to scribble out a section of a plan which no longer makes sense, whilst others will find this messiness distracting and will struggle to move on productively. The checklist below might help you to avoid some common planning pitfalls:

 CHECKLIST

- Think about the size of the paper you use: some planners prefer to use large, flipchart-size sheets of paper, others are happier with smaller, A4 sheets; I have occasionally come across scholars who prefer to begin with small, 4″ x 6″ cards, but these are usually reserved for later in the process.
- Colour and size of pen also matters more than you might expect. A normal ballpoint pen used on a piece of flipchart paper can look mean spirited and half-hearted. Some people prefer to use coloured pens to indicate different points on a plan; others find this distracting.
- You will notice that I am assuming a hand-drawn plan here, which is another decision for you to make. Generally, I find that plans written by hand, rather than being computer generated, are more memorable and have a human quality which I find encouraging; you may differ, so try both means before deciding which suits you best.
- As you plan, it is worth noticing how you respond to mistakes. If you find scribbling out across a plan distressing, or new pieces of plan inserted around older ideas distracting, it can be a good idea to use cards or sticky notes on your plan so that you can change their position readily without making a mess of your plan. Similarly, you might find it quicker simply to throw a plan away and start afresh rather than trying neatly to erase some sections in order to revise them.
- If you are working in a group to give a presentation, decide in advance which planning method suits everyone (and be prepare to veto a planning method if you know that it is one which tends to confuse you rather than being helpful) and be ready to meet to plan (if you can) rather than working online if you know that computer-generated plans are not helpful to you.

Although I am using a spider chart in this guide, there are many other planning methods available to you, each with advantages and potential disadvantages, but one criterion remains true of them all: know how far you can push your plan. A good plan is one which uses a method which suits both how your mind works and the material under discussion (for most presentations a spider chart is the preferable option) but it is also one which is as simple, or as complex, as you are happy to make it.

The spider chart I have shown you here would make perfect sense to me. More colour and I would be distracted, but others might prefer to introduce a new colour for each section of the presentation, or use two colours denoting the advantages and disadvantages of the options being considered. Symbols, too, are useful to some in their planning, whilst others prefer just to use words. There are scholars who would use arrows to connect different aspects of their plan; I would find myself getting lost at that point. So, as you work through the plan for your presentation, ask yourself at each stage whether the materials you are using (paper size, pen colour and size, sticky notes or not) are working for you and whether the plan is as complicated, or more complicated, than you would like it to be. For most of us, once we have found a comfortable way to plan effectively we will rest there and tend to stick to what we know works best for us.

Planning as a thinking tool

You will have noticed that the plan which has developed during this chapter has become more than just a means to arrange some pieces of information. It has allowed me to think about what I want to say at a deeper level. What matters to me in disseminating this material? What are my essential points? What are my fundamental questions? How do I expect the audience to respond? What do I hope to gain from this experience? Where do I still need to go to complete the project?

If you can approach planning from this perspective, seeing it as a way to give you the space to think and arrange your thoughts and needs rather than just arranging material, you will be in a much stronger position once you come to present. Ideally, once you stand up in front of an audience you will not be considering these questions at all – they will all have been answered in the planning; this will leave your head brilliantly clear, allowing you to focus on the occasion itself and the relationship you want to form with the audience.

Planning as a communication tool

If you are hoping to gain some useful initial feedback on your idea for a presentation, or you would like some more detailed opinions about your developed thoughts, you will find planning invaluable. If you give a colleague or mentor little more than a sketchy idea of where you might go in your presentation, your intentions could be entirely misunderstood. Time and goodwill can be wasted as you gain feedback which is irrelevant to your actual intentions, and your colleague is left confused and having to work too hard to support you. If, later, you show colleagues your perfectly prepared and written up paper, they may be reluctant to suggest that you take out or rewrite a whole section or more of a paper which you have clearly spent time and effort producing.

If you show your plan to your supporters, you will have the best of both worlds. It is formed enough, and depicted clearly enough, that it can be commented upon with confidence by your colleagues, who will also feel happy to suggest that you remove or revise whole sections of the plan. Your response to these suggestions will also be more positive, as reworking a plan as a result of constructive criticism is not hugely time consuming or diffi-cult and is certainly easier than the effort involved in revising a written-up paper or polished presentation. By taking this approach the revisions which you implement might show you new areas of exploration or other areas which, in the light of the comments you have received on other aspects of your presentation, you would like to revisit.

Planning as a control tool

A conference is intended to be a forum for the productive exchange of ideas and information and your contribution will therefore be prepared in the spirit of scholarly sharing and exploration. However, you will naturally want to ensure that, whilst the event is interesting for others, it is also of maximum benefit to you; planning can help you to achieve this. In the spider chart produced in this chapter I have tried to create a balance between giving out information about cake making and the conclusions I have already reached about what I intend to do, and questions and con-cerns which I still have and want to share with the audience.

I am not suggesting here that you can expect to dictate the questions you receive, but I would urge you to think about which questions you would prefer to receive, and which topics would be of most value to you in the ensuing discussion. Unless many of its members have already planned a question in advance of the event, an audience is very likely to respond positively to comments I make such as 'I haven't decided yet whether or not to ice the cake' or 'I am not sure whether or not the recipient is veg-etarian; perhaps someone here today will know'. You are not precluding the possibility of an unexpected question such as 'Is the child lactose intoler-ant?', but you are certainly giving a useful steer to the audience who will generally appreciate it.

TOP TIP

By the time your plan has reached this stage you might have forgotten your initial six-point plan altogether and this is unlikely to be a problem. However, now is a good time to check back to it just in case you suddenly realise that you have overlooked a section of your presentation which you had originally meant to include and which would still be useful. I sometimes find at this point that I do not want to change my whole plan, but I do want to add a point to the introduction or conclusions section which I had overlooked as the plan became more detailed and exciting.

The benefits of a clock chart

You may have noticed on the spider chart that I have not assigned any order to the points I want to make. I am content enough that they are the right points, but have not yet decided exactly which order would suit my presentation best. In most cases this would be easily resolved: as I move from planning to preparing the presentation in more detail things could naturally fall into place. If, for example, I am describing a chronological process I would have an order imposed upon my material, especially if I was producing slides which included diagrams such as timelines or flow charts.

However, there are occasions when no obvious order emerges, and at these times a clock chart can help. To produce a clock chart you just draw the outline of a clock face on a piece of paper:

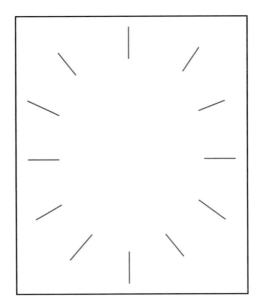

You would then go back to your spider chart and transfer the main headings to the clock chart, deciding as you go along on the best order for them:

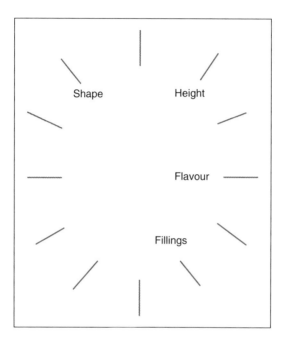

 TOP TIP

It helps if you leave the introduction and conclusions sections off the clock chart at this stage, so that you are not constrained. Once you have decided on the order of the main points of your presentation, you can then add 'introduction' and 'conclusions' to the chart.

 TOP TIP

Leaving a few gaps between the main points allows you to complicate it later, if you like, by adding some of the subsections of your presentation in the spaces between your main points.

Your clock chart will end up looking like this:

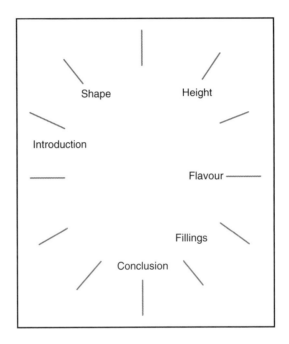

 TOP TIP

You are quite likely to change your mind about the best order for your material, so try using sticky notes with the main points on and moving them around or, if you prefer, make several copies of your clock chart outline so that you can keep throwing them away if they do not seem to be working well, moving on easily to the next iteration of the chart.

 TOP TIP

If you find that you tend to lose energy as you work though a project such as preparing a paper or presentation, or if you flag as you rehearse, a clock chart can keep you inspired. As you work through, you are not talking in a vacuum: you can see how many 'hours' you have left to go on the clock chart.

Mode of presentation

There is now a decision to make, one which might already have been made for you by the conference organisers. Is this to be the giving of a paper, or a full-blown presentation? If it is to be a paper, you are almost there: you can now write it out in full, remembering to use spoken English where possible rather than a formal, written English style. As I mentioned earlier, you might want to add a few notes to yourself in the margins of your script such as 'slow down', 'smile' or 'halfway through'. You will also need to mark the places at which you could safely go off script for a few moments to elaborate on a particular point. You would then be able to move straight through to the rehearsal stage.

However, most scholars will be expected, or will want, to enliven their material with presentation aids; many would prefer to stand rather than sit when reading a paper; and most would expect to offer some supporting material in the form of handouts or similar. With this in mind, I would suggest that you work through the next couple of chapters, which are concerned chiefly with presentations. Of course, if your conference organisers, or your discipline generally, expect a presentation, the next few chapters will be essential reading.

Eight
PRESENTATION AIDS

Presentations aids appear in this guide about halfway through, and this is a deliberate placement. It is not until about halfway through the process of preparing to present, after the first few rehearsals, that you would need to think about them: earlier, and you risk ascribing far too much importance to them; later, and you might struggle to fit them seamlessly into your presentation. The 'your' in that last sentence is important: *you* are the only presentation aid you really need – anything else can be useful and stimulating, but not vital. It can be difficult to think of presentations in this way when we have all become used to slick-looking presentations through data projectors, but it is important that you do view it like this. In that way you will focus initially on the most important aspects of the presentation, the material, the message, the structure. You will then be able to consider the best use of presentation aids to support all of these before you return to your role and work on your dissemination techniques until you are confident that you will be giving the best possible view of the material.

You have a whole host of presentation aids at your command and you will be familiar with many of them, either as a user or audience member, so I will not spend huge amounts of your time here going through each of them in minute detail; instead, I will be asking you to think more strategically about how to make the most of them. Before we get started on that though, a checklist with a brief word on the most common presentation aids might be useful.

 CHECKLIST

1 **Blackboard, whiteboard, flipchart:** freely available and can be used spontaneously; there is no lasting record of the activity unless you take a photo of it for distribution.
2 **Data projector, slide projector, overhead projector (OHP):** commonly available and professional looking; subject to technical problems so have a back-up ready.

3 **Interactive whiteboard (smartboard):** excellent as long as you have the technical skills to make it work well; can be time consuming to set up on the day.

4 **Handouts:** the prefect old-fashioned standby if things go wrong, also great for takeaway material or used during Q & A; just because they are traditional aids, do not allow them to be boring and amateur.

5 **Virtual learning environment (VLE):** useful if you have material lodged there which could support either your presentation or Q & A; make sure that you can gain remote access easily.

6 **Wikis and online polling systems:** these can add immediacy and excitement if they are created as part of an event and shown on a screen behind the speaker; keep a firm control on them (ideally through an assistant) so that no inappropriate messages are displayed.

7 **Demonstration:** audiences tend to enjoy the human scale appeal of a demonstration and it can be memorable and impressive; make sure, if you can, that you film it in advance in case the demonstration fails, so that you can show the film instead.

8 **Film and audio:** both can bring your subject area alive, as long as you have timed them in advance so that you know they will work well within your timing; be sure to embed them within your data projector slides, if you have them, and have a back-up plan ready in case the technology fails on the day.

9 **Online resources and mobile phones:** as with video and audio, make the use of online resources as smooth as possible by hyperlinking from your presentation slides or opening up the web pages you need in advance of the presentation and minimising them ready for use; mobile phones can be useful if you are asking people to tweet as you present but never assume that everyone will have a mobile phone with internet access.

10 **Your audience:** not the most obvious visual aid, perhaps, but potentially important nonetheless if you are going to ask for a show of hands, or for feedback, or for a volunteer; only involve audience members if you feel confident about their response.

Having outlined in brief the aids at your disposal, we can now move on to consider how best to employ them.

Some golden rules

- Use no less than a 20-point font on a visual aid; use a sans serif font (Calibri and Arial work well).
- Try to include most of the material in the top two-thirds of the projected image.
- Leave plenty of space around images.
- Never photocopy an extract onto a handout unless it is important to have an exact facsimile: take the time to retype material if necessary.
- If you include dense material, such as an extract copied from a book or newspaper onto a slide, you would not expect the audience members to be able to read it from the screen. You need to make this clear, explaining that you just want them to be able to see a particular layout of material.

- Avoid font colours which are hard to see on your chosen background colour (red, for example, is notoriously difficult on a screen but perfectly acceptable on a handout).
- Always check out your presentation aid design in context to see how it would work for a real audience.
- Be as sparing as possible with the material: masses of impenetrable material just will not work.
- Audience members should never feel rushed: read through the material you are offering them as you rehearse to make sure that you have the right quantity of material; on the day, read through it silently as they do so that you get your timing right.
- If you feel that a greater quantity of material is needed than you have time for, include it on a handout but use it as takeaway material, referring the audience to it only during the question and answer session or at the close of your presentation slot.
- Never, ever, just read out loud what you have written from a screen: the presentation aid is the audience's support material, not your script.

Heat and light levels

Using any type of technology can be heat producing, so make sure that the room will not become too stuffy as a result of the technology you are using. If the room is quite small, or the audience unexpectedly large, be bold and open a window either at the start of your talk or in a break before your presentation slot.

Air-conditioning problems can creep up on your during a presentation. Whilst you would not want your audience to feel chilly, a slightly cooler than normal atmosphere is preferable to enduring air conditioning which is set to allow too high a temperature. Take it upon yourself to check the temperature setting and change it if you feel that it is too high. If you are told that it is centrally controlled for a building, consider turning it off altogether and/or opening a window if you feel that the room will become stuffy. The time it takes to give a presentation is quite enough for a comfortably warm room to become overheated, so erring on the side of pleasantly cool works best.

There is an understandable tendency in a presentation to become anxious about the visibility of your visual aids. This might have you closing blinds and turning down light levels, or turning off the lights altogether. This is often a mistake. It is usually easy enough to see what is on a screen without any alteration in light levels, unless it is an especially bright day, so be strategic. Turning down the lights can be a pleasingly dramatic moment in a presentation, heightening the audience's sense of expectation, but it does mean that you are less visible. Given that you are the presenter and so the most important visual aid there could be, you will want to minimise the time that you are not fully visible to the audience. As with other aspects of presentation aids try out the light levels before the event. Even if you cannot do this in situ, you can get a good idea in advance of the light level needed to make the presentation aid effective and then replicate that for your presentation.

The audience is in the best position to judge this, so if you are in any doubt at all, ask the audience members whether the light level works for them. Even better, have a colleague in the audience who you have primed to give a firm answer to any practical questions such as this: that way, you can be sure of an accurate answer and you will not waste time worrying.

Availability of technology

It perhaps goes without saying that you cannot assume anything with regard to technology. Most conference venues would, of course, have full technology facilities available. However, if you are in a breakout room, chairing a panel discussion, or if you are giving a poster presentation in a large hall, or if yours is one of six, small, parallel sessions, you cannot be absolutely certain that technology will be available, so it makes sense always to check in advance.

If you are told that 'full tech' is available, make sure that your 'full tech' is the same as theirs. Overhead projectors, for example, are still useful presentation aids in some circumstances, yet many organisations simply will not have a single overhead projector on site. Slide projectors, too, are less available than you might expect, mainly because people tend to include images in data projector slideshows now rather than using the more old-fashioned image slide that requires a traditional projector.

Assuming that every form of technology has full internet access, or that computers and internet systems never crash, can lead you into the frustrating situation of having stored your presentation slideshow in a cloud or having emailed it to yourself, only to find that you cannot access it in the conference room. Although you will probably be able to find another room from which to access and then save it onto the internal system of the conference organisers, this will leave you feeling rather foolish and exhausted with nerves.

Once you have thought about it like this, prevention is easy. Always carry your presentation with you in a saved format which you can access without the internet (never will the humble memory stick be more important to you than at this moment) and, if your entire presentation relies on internet access, make sure that you have something else prepared as a back-up plan.

 TOP TIP

If you are caught out in this way, ignore the almost irresistible urge to complain about it throughout your presentation. Bemoaning the situation and repeatedly referring to the brilliance of the presentation you could have shown if only you had access to the internet will turn the audience's sympathy rapidly to irritation.

Practicalities

You will probably expect to present fairly much anywhere you are put, and this is the best attitude to have. However, it will help your audience if you take command of the practicalities of the situation. The first of these is timing: making it clear to the audience members how you will conduct your presentation slot will set you off together on the right footing. Even though they will have information in the delegate pack, they will still appreciate being told exactly how long your paper or presentation will be, and how long they have for questions and answers. Of course, for a smaller event there may be no delegate pack or printed itinerary and, even if there is, people easily seem to lose this type of material.

The audience members will also want to know what you expect of them: is it a question and answer session they are being offered, or a forum for discussion? If you are using handouts as your presentation aid, when will these be given out? Will more material be offered to them at the end of the presentation slot?

It also helps if you can take control of the space. If you are including a demonstration, be prepared to create a platform high enough for each audience member to see what is going on. If the seating is arranged in a way that feels awkward to you, consider spending a few moments asking everyone to move to a new format (if the audience is small enough to make this practicable). As you are the primary presentation aid, make sure that your working space is comfortable. It is not at all unusual to see a speaker walking back and forth across a stage or similar platform, having to move around a stray chair at every turn and never thinking to move it: this makes the audience want to shout out loud at you, so take a minute or two in making sure that the presentation space is as good as you can make it before you commence.

Before you begin to speak, you might want to take a quick look around to see if any of the conference organisers are actually in the room. That way, if anything should go wrong, you will know exactly where to look. Similarly, check the lectern or presentation table, or beside the light switches or data projector switch, to see if there is a phone number given for technical support. This might not help you much if the event is at the weekend, but it is worth a try as long as you have not had to waste too much time trying to find the number.

Visibility

Having mentioned colour in general terms, it is also worth mentioning colour and font impact for those audience members with any type of visual impairment. I tend to keep a copy of my notes, handouts and presentation slides near me on a memory stick and an email attachment so that I can send it on to anyone who asks, or increase/alter the font setting and print out large print and/or black and white copies on the day for any audience members who have found the font size or lettering/background contrast irksome.

Audience members can also cut down their useful view of your presentation aids without meaning to make this mistake. This might be because you were sitting right at the front of the stage waiting to be introduced and they failed to notice that you were going to have to walk back six paces to the screen. Alternatively, some audience members might have come into the room talking to friends and not noticed that their seats were behind a pillar. Even something as simple as being stuck behind someone very tall can cause unexpected problems if you are showing a demonstration at table height in the front of the room. Luckily, the solutions to visibility problems lie with you. If you can, make sure that you sit near the screen you will be using at the outset of the event, and ask members of the audience if they can see clearly before you begin to talk. Show that you take this seriously by encouraging any audience members who you can see will have difficultly to move; people are sometimes hesitant about moving once they are seated, so a little gentle encouragement can be very welcome.

Although poor visibility is the most obvious problem you might expect to face, over-visibilty can also be a problem and it might not be something a presenter would notice until it is too late. In some large lecture/conference rooms there will be several screens, each showing the images which you want to see projected. The difficulty this can create is that your audience is no longer looking just at you and the screen behind you, but might be looking away from you altogether staring at a screen which is nearer to them but a long way from you. This might not matter to you but, again, you need to take control. In many cases this just does not work, as the audience becomes fractured and fails to recognise you as its primary focus. Turning off all but one screen is usually easy enough to do, so take this option if you feel it would help you to present your material most effectively.

Nerves

Although I will be discussing the best way to control and use your nerves productively later in this guide, we need to consider here the relationship between your nerves and your presentation aids. Seeing a shaking hand can be off-putting for an audience, which is one of several reasons why you might avoid speaking from a script on a piece of paper, where shaking hands are obvious. If you are giving a demonstration, a shaking hand will be far less distracting as the audience's attention will soon focus on the demonstration rather than you.

If you are using a data projector and you know you are likely to be more nervous than you would like, you might consider using the keyboard to move from slide to slide, rather than using a hand-held gadget. This prevents you moving ahead by mistake and also helps you to avoid the temptation to point the infrared light at the screen in a rather manic fashion in order to try to make your point. Unless you have an excellent reason for doing so, a pre-timed slideshow which is out of your control is best avoided for a presentation.

 TOP TIP

No audience is so stupid that it needs you to use a pointer (either a manual or infrared version) to point out text on the screen: we can all read what it is you want us to absorb. If you think your audience might not find the point you want to make, you have put too much text on the screen: break it up and use several slides if you need to, but never point to words on the screen. Instead, use a pointer exclusively for pointing out *detail* in the images (not the whole image, which is obvious) and it should always be used sparingly.

Even those presenters who are comfortable with technology can lose their way if they have given themselves an overly complicated set up for their presentation, with a data projector slideshow and separate film and audio clips or web pages to find. As with much else, practise not only makes perfect, it also allows you to gauge your limitations. Although the adrenalin on the day will generally sharpen your mind and improve your performance, if you have tripped over the technology at every rehearsal, give serious thought to simplifying how you disseminate the information.

Some presenters are more than comfortable with technology: they are enamoured of it to such an extent that they can no longer see its pitfalls. There is little more irritating than a presenter who whizzes through a series of dense slides and complicated web pages leaving the audience behind within seconds and never offering time to catch up. If you suspect that you are one of these presenters, always make sure that you show a less technically enthused colleague or mentor your presentation before you give it live to an audience.

 TOP TIP

In terms of complexity of material, the general rule is easy: unless you have very good reason for producing something complicated (such as showing the capabilities of new software, for example) then keep it simple. If you want to demonstrate the greenness of an apple, just hold up an apple (and then make sure that you have a picture in hard copy and on a data projector in case you leave the apple on a train on the way to the conference). If what you want to show is inherently hugely complex, put the detail on a handout but also produce a simplified version from which you can speak.

Boredom levels

Naturally, you will find your topic area riveting, and you can reasonably expect that your audience will be intrigued too. This curiosity can be developed during your talk such that by the end of it your audience is eager to ask questions and impressed with your work. This can only be achieved, however, if you can keep the audience's attention throughout the event. Much of the work we have done in this chapter will help you with this: your audience will now be in the best seating pattern with the most conducive light levels in the optimum temperature. However, one thing is beyond your immediate control: what happened to them before your paper or presentation.

If your slot is just after lunch, you will probably already be aware from your own experience that you will have an uphill job to retain everyone's interest for all of your paper or presentation. If you are not in a position to change slots, there really is no point in trying to bully audience members into being as alert as they were before lunch. Instead, aim to keep them pleasantly entertained for your presentation slot and then give them plenty of material to take away in the form of a handout or additional hard copy material. Offer them a reasonable amount of interactivity (asking for a show of hands in response to a proposition, for example), interesting graphics in your presentation as opposed to text only slides and perhaps a brief video or audio insert. Whatever you do, refuse to be downhearted if you feel that some audience members' attention is flagging at some points: this is human nature and not a personal slight.

 TOP TIP

I have been referring in this section to takeaway material on the assumption that, most usually, this would be a handout. However, if you have reams of material that you would like your audience to be able to peruse at leisure, you could produce an eye-catching postcard with some very brief information on it and a clearly set out website reference or series of references so that audience members can go to your project website or your personal/professional web-page, or to any other site you think would be helpful after the event.

Whether or not you are being asked to speak directly after lunch will be obvious from the programme and is a well-known challenge for presenters. What will be less obvious to you is what the audience will have experienced in the sessions directly before yours, but this too could have an impact on your choice of presentation aids. If there are several papers or presentations in a row without a break, you can expect to have a tired audience, and might take some time opening windows and/or suggesting that the audience might like to take just a few minutes to stand up and stretch. Be firm here: at the end of the three or four minutes you stipulated you will need to get started, even if one or two people have not yet returned.

If you are aware that the speakers before you are all giving glossy data projector presentations, you might consider moving away from that form of presentation aid altogether, if your material would allow you to do this. Similarly, if you are in a group presentation you will need to discuss within your group whether you are all going to use one slideshow or whether you are each going to produce your own, or whether in fact you might choose to have only some members of the group using a slideshow.

If this seems to be becoming a little downbeat, it is worth remembering that, for most of the presentations and papers you give, boredom will not be an issue at all. If it is, I hope it has become clear in this section that the problem is unlikely to be of your making and is countered by some relatively easy to implement measures.

What is far less easy to counteract, and is likely to become an increasing problem with some of the newer data projector slideshow software packages on the market, is the opposite of boredom: the visual and mental overstimulation that can cause real problems for the unwary speaker. You might reasonably assume that an audience would thoroughly enjoy a presentation which shows flashing images, flying text and loud music, or that one way to hold an audience's attention would be to zoom it from one section of a presentation to another by means of advanced technology. You might already have spotted the problems implied here. Too much information is just disheartening; flashing images can induce epilepsy; flying text is very difficult for visually impaired or dyslexic audience members; loud music can be off-putting for those with hearing disorders, and going from one section to another by means of whizzing the audience across a slide as another emerges in the background can cause severe vertigo. This is serious stuff, and although you might not be able to avoid it altogether, at least bear these issues in mind as you prepare your presentation aids.

 TOP TIP

The 'slow reveal' presentation slideshow should be used with the utmost caution. If you set up every one of your slides in such a way that each line of text only appears with an additional click of the mouse, keyboard or hand-held pointer, you risk two problems. First, you will have to know every single line of your slides off by heart (and know that your nerves will never get the better of you) to avoid the moment of horrible surprise when you think you are moving to the next slide and a stray last line of the slide appears. Second, if there is no good reason for the slow reveal your audience members are unlikely to sit with bated breath waiting for your next reveal; they are more likely to feel slightly patronised.

Flipped learning

It is currently rather fashionable in educational settings for academics to make use of 'flipped learning' or the 'flipped classroom'. In this system, students are given information before a lecture slot (either in the form of written or online material or, more usually, through a film or podcast), the lecture slot then being used for a question and answer session about the material. To some extent, the same principle is being applied to those events where speakers are asked to provide a copy of their paper for distribution before the event.

In theory, this allows the audience to become familiar with material before you present. However, it would be highly unusual for your presentation slot to be no more than questions and answers (although if it were a panel or round-table discussion this might be the case). It would be unlikely that you would want to work from exactly the same material as you gave out; although this would be possible it might be a little tedious for those who have already studied the material. Instead, make sure you have copies of the paper to hand for those who do not have a copy with them, then use a slideshow or handout to summarise the main points. In that way everyone is at roughly the same point of understanding before you delve into questions or a discussion. I have seen presenters who have taken this further and produced a final slide which lists some possible areas for discussion and this can work well as long as you are prepared to abandon the pre-prepared questions in favour of those which are raised by the audience at the time.

Formality

It is tempting to work upon the assumption that the more formal and slicker your presentation aids, the better they will be at any event. Although this is largely true, there are exceptions. If, for example, you are disseminating your material at an intimate gathering of no more than half a dozen fellow researchers, such as might happen at a small research seminar, then a full data projector presentation might be seen as so out of keeping with the event that you risk social awkwardness and also, interestingly, a certain amount of suspicion.

You might expect that your fellow seminar members might be impressed and perhaps a little flattered at the effort you have so clearly made, but it is also possible that they will think you are hiding insubstantial amounts of material beyond an ostentatious presentation. Be gentle with this situation: if the seminar is a regular event which is most usually conducted on an informal basis, you might want to follow the norm. If you are going to use more adventurous presentation aids, explain at the beginning why you are doing this (you would like to try them out before a conference, for example, or you think they will help make a particular section of material clearer) so as to reassure your audience; a presentation aid is only an aid if it actually helps you in what you are trying to achieve.

Timing

Using presentation aids takes a surprisingly long time – far longer than you might expect. You will have noticed, probably with exasperation, when a speaker at an event you have attended has rushed through a slide, not giving you enough time to read and understand it. You are unlikely to have noticed (why would you?) the length of time another speaker has had to stand by, patiently waiting whilst the audience absorbs the information before moving on to the next part of a talk. In the later chapter on delivering your material this will be explored in more detail, but for now I would like to suggest that you always plan, rehearse and revise your material taking into account the fact that you will lose speaking time with each presentation aid you offer. This is generally a good thing, given that many of your audience members will assimilate information visually more readily than aurally, but it does need to be taken into consideration at every stage of your preparation.

Timing will also have a direct effect on the number and type of presentation aids you use. If you want to include, for example, a data projector slide show and a demonstration and a handout to which you will be referring, this will obviously take longer than using just one aid to illustrate the material. Equally, if your slides are very complicated they will take up more time. If in rehearsal you are running over on time, avoid the ready solution of simply speeding up your talking pace; instead simplify the material on your slides or reduce the number of slides. If you know that you will not need to refer to slides for a few minutes during the presentation, consider including a blank slide so that the audience is not left looking at an old slide; you might also think of including a 'hidden' slide which would be used only if you need to add material at the last minute.

 TOP TIP

No audience member is happy to see a slide or two whizz by as you click forward because you are running over on time. This is especially true if you explain, as you gallop through, that you would have loved to share this material but you have no time to do it. If you feel, after a few rehearsals, that the timing of the presentation cannot be predicted with any accuracy (perhaps the material you are sharing is complicated or will be entirely new to the audience and so will need more or less explaining depending on its reaction on the day), then include a few slides which could be condensed into no more than a few words or expanded to fill several minutes productively; that way nobody knows that they have missed anything and you are never at a loss for useful visual material.

Handouts can be a particular challenge in terms of their timing, so it helps to plan in advance how you are going to use this particular presentation aid. There are several ways you might do this:

 CHECKLIST

1 **In advance:** if your handout material is essential to understanding your presentation you might want to send it to audience members in advance. However, this could be taken as presumptuous (they are busy people) or rather ponderous (surely you could just explain at the event?), so only do this if you know that the material will be received with enthusiasm. Make sure that additional copies are available on the day, ideally some time before your paper or presentation. Leaving copies in a central point, clearly labelled as the handouts for your presentation slot, might help you to reach audience members who are attending a parallel session and so would not otherwise come across your material.

2 **At the opening:** starting distribution of your handouts as soon as people begin to settle is preferable to waiting for silence and then handing them around. If your presentation slot is after a break you would ideally leave piles of the handout at the ends of rows and ask people to pick up a copy as they return to their seats. People become flustered if you begin to talk even before they have a copy of the handout, so you will need to be patient despite your nerves.

3 **During your paper or presentation:** this is rarely a good idea. The time it takes to circulate handouts can ruin the flow of your talk and will certainly waste presenting time. One solution seems to be to ask the audience members in that break for circulation if they are clear so far, or if they have any questions, but you then risk them being frustrated as they try to read the handout whilst also listening to the discussion taking place. You might also be in peril of losing control of the timing altogether. The only way I have ever seen this done with any success is when the speaker gives out a handout which is replicated on a slide on the screen, so everyone can be looking at that as the speaker talks through it and the handouts are circulated; these can then be referred to repeatedly as the event progresses and the slideshow moves on.

4 **At the Q & A stage:** some caution would be necessary here. A list of questions you think the audience would like to ask you might not be well received. Suggested areas for debate can work, as long as you also allow time and space for other questions leading to alternative areas of discussion. What can be very useful, however, is a handout with some additional information on, especially complicated facts and figures. These could include material which you have already given briefly in the presentation but to which you suspect the audience might like to return. You might not use the handout at all, but it is impressive if, in response to an audience question, you can assure delegates that you can provide the relevant facts and figures on a handout which you will leave for them to pick up at the end. If you expect to have to refer to some part of the handout during the Q & A section of your slot, copy it onto a slide which is lodged after the last slide of your presentation proper, ready to move onto it so that it can be discussed as you distribute the handout.

5   **As a discussion document:** this is a little different from a Q & A handout; you will not be imparting facts through a handout but rather listing some suggestions for discussion, perhaps with some facts and figures or document extracts alongside those suggestions. You would have told the audience in advance that the document was going to circulate at the close of the paper or presentation but that it is only a suggestion document, not a script for discussion. This would only tend to be produced if the audience was small enough to allow discussion to flow freely and within the allotted time and so distribution would not be too time consuming. There might be occasions when you would think it appropriate to hand out the document at the start of the paper or presentation, so as to guide the audience through the entire event ready for the discussion session. However, you would still want to reassure the audience that the handout was for guidance and support rather than an instruction as to what could be discussed.

6   **At the close:** if you feel it would be helpful for the audience to take away a handout, either with a copy of the key points from your paper or presentation or with some additional material, leave these in a pile at the back of the room and make known their availability. Trying to hand them around as the audience is trying to leave for the next event or a refreshment break risks a confusing end to your successful event.

 TOP TIP

Be wary of printing out a list of your slides with lines for notes beside them. Although the presentation software allows you to do this, only produce this type of handout if you are happy for your audience to see the entire slideshow before you have said a single word.

Post-event impact

We tend to think of presentation aids as simply supporting the presentation itself, but they can also support your professional image and increase the impact of your paper or presentation. I have mentioned several ways that this might be achieved throughout this chapter; I have brought them together here as a checklist for you to consider:

 CHECKLIST

1   On your last slide put your name and email address: that way people can make a note for future reference without having the embarrassment of admitting that they have forgotten either.

2   A postcard advertising your project, with a website address and your email address, can be placed on each seat before delegates enter the room, or can be offered at the end of the presentation.

(Continued)

(Continued)

3   A handout with the key points of your presentation is a useful attachment to any other handout you are using. If this is also one of the first slides you use in the presentation, it will have even more impact.

4   If you are offering an ephemeral presentation aid, such as a video or audio clip, make sure that the audience knows where to go to view it again.

5   Similarly with a demonstration: film it in advance, upload the film to the internet and offer the link to it in a handout or on screen (leaving enough time for everyone to copy it down accurately).

6   If you use an interactive whiteboard (smartboard), save any documents you create so that you can send them to delegates or lodge them somewhere electronically.

7   Any form of event production which will spill over after the event needs to be captured. Online polling is an excellent example of this. It can have an immediate impact, but the result will change over days or perhaps weeks, so a website will need to be updated regularly so that interested delegates can return to the results over time.

8   If you are asked an unexpected question and your response is to offer to email your considered view after the event, remember that it might not have been only that questioner who was interested in this aspect of your research. Offering to email your response to any delegate who is interested will show a pleasing willingness to engage and will increase your network of contacts.

9   If Twitter is being used as part of the event dissemination, you need to keep an eye on it both during and after the event. Even if you do not want to tweet anything yourself, you will want to know what is being said about the material you have shared at the event.

10   The best talks are those where there is a sense of a genuine conversation, even if time does not allow this to be as lengthy as you would like. It is so common for discussions to be cut short though lack of time that you might want to consider setting up a chat room prior to your talk, or a wiki or blog, so that interested audience members can carry on the conversation for as long as they like after the event.

As you can gather, presentation aids are not simple but they can be hugely effective in helping you to get your message across and they are often fun to produce. Once you have prepared them you can move on to the next challenge: preparing yourself for the event ahead.

Nine
PREPARING TO PRESENT

There are two approaches to presentation preparation which might be tempting, but rarely work. The first is to learn a script off by heart, word for word, and then try to replicate that script on the day. There are a couple of reasons why this is likely to fail: first, you will have written, to some extent, in formal language which sounds strange when you use it in a speaking situation. Second, if you once lose your place you will struggle to find a way back to the memorised script; this can be disastrous.

I recently gave a presentation at a prestigious event alongside an academic who I have always admired. He told me with great confidence the night before the presentations that he would spend the evening memorising his script. I was clearly startled, and he explained with some pride that he always does this, and what others think of as effortlessly delivered prose is actually just hard work and a good memory. However, my admiration was short-lived. The next day he began his presentation – and was unexpectedly interrupted after the first minute with a minor question about the first point he had made. He never recovered and spent the rest of his time slot clearly struggling to make his points succinctly whilst desperately trying to remember what they actually were. A salutary lesson in how not to present.

The second approach is largely a myth, circulated by those who claim that they do it. You will probably come across presenters who tell you that preparation is an overrated activity; indeed, some might suggest that preparation positively puts them off their stroke when it comes to presenting. They will claim that they just jot down a few notes and then happily work from these, extemporising as they go and amazing an audience with their fluency, wit and insight. Having been on the receiving end of presentations such as these, I can see the problem. The presenters are so energised by adrenalin, so overly sure of their abilities, that they simply cannot see how poorly they are presenting or how unenthusiastic is the response to their efforts.

They might also, of course, be shying away from the absolute truth. There are presenters who find their flagging confidence is boosted by an assurance to all that the words simply trip off their tongue. They might be allowed this indulgence, but I want to work with you on a fail-safe way to prepare, one which will allow you to give your best possible performance. As you grow more confident, and I can guarantee that this will come with experience, you may change this routine a little, perhaps adding in your own preparation tricks or simplifying it in places. This will be to the good, but for now following the routine offered here would be advisable.

The process is based on six rehearsals and assumes that you will work from a full script in the first instance, working it down into prompts as you go. Again, with experience this might change and what I refer to here as a 'full script' might become, for you, no more than a series of detailed bullet-pointed items, and this would be fine. It all depends what works best for you as your presentation aptitude develops. The six stages are these:

 CHECKLIST

1 script for content and timing;
2 script for timing only;
3 prompts for content and timing;
4 reduced prompts for presentation aids;
5 prompts and aids for impact;
6 final rehearsal for confidence.

I will explain each of these as we go, offering suggestions as to how you can use each step of the process to best effect. Each stage will be, in effect, a full rehearsal of your presentation, although the early rehearsals could be a little disjointed and might not feel much like a presentation.

 TOP TIP

If you are presenting as a group, you might like to do the first two rehearsals listed here as individuals, and then come together as a group from rehearsal three onwards. You might need to include one extra rehearsal as an initial run through to ensure that you are each working at the same stage of readiness as you begin to rehearse together as a group.

1. Rehearsal with script for content and timing

This is the first point at which you may vary your routine as time goes on and your confidence grows. In the early days of your life as a presenter, you may choose to write out a full script of what you want to say in your presentation. This is certainly a safe way to ensure that you feel comfortable with the material you are using; it also gives you a good sense of whether your argument flows. What it is less likely to give you is a precise idea of how the timing will work, partly because you are reading out loud and so will almost certainly be speedier than you would be if you were looking up at an audience and speaking without a script, partly because you have not yet included any visual aids.

For a 20-minute presentation I would always urge a presenter to aim for 17–18 minutes in the final rehearsal. At this stage, given how long presentation aids take to use, and assuming that you were just using a data projector slideshow presentation, I would advise you to aim for about 15 minutes. Of course, if you are planning to give a demonstration or use external material such as a film or audio clips, these can be timed accurately and taken off this 15 minutes for every 20 minutes of presentation.

During this first run-through, try not to be put off if you falter for much of the time, or if you realise as you go through that your plan has not converted into the perfect script. Instead, be confident that this will work out in the end and be ruthless; a red pen in your hand as you talk, be ready to cross out any sections which are unnecessary or to put a large star in the margin where you think it works well, and a question mark in the margin where it does not feel right.

 TOP TIP

In talking about a rehearsal or a run-through here, I mean for you to stand up and give the full presentation in the form it has reached at each step. So, for this run through it would be reading the script aloud, looking up every now and then as if to make eye contact with the audience and trying to pause for effect as you would in a full presentation. If you simply read through silently in your head, or even read aloud but sitting down looking at your script, your timing will not be accurate and you will lose the chance to get a feel for how the presentation will develop.

Post-rehearsal activity

You are now ready to amend your script. However tempting it is to second guess the decisions you made as you spoke, do not let yourself do this.

Instead, cut out the sections which you now know must go and rewrite those sections which were not as good as you would want. If you are a little over on time, this cutting process will be wholly productive and so you can feel good about it. If you are a little under on time, search through to see if there is somewhere you could usefully explain a point more fully or expand an argument to good effect.

It is possible (indeed, it is relatively common) to find at this stage that you have more material than you need. I always find this heartening. It means that I am keen to share my work with others and I am now in a strong position, able to take out material and leave only the best behind. If I were significantly over on time I would go back to my plan. Clearly my mistake would have been made earlier in the process, before I made the script. I would reassess my plan (and probably ask a colleague to help me with this) and then simply remove a whole section, or a subsection from some of my sections. I have usually found that editing out a whole section leaves me with a stronger presentation than if I tinker with each section, which could leave me with too superficial a presentation.

 TOP TIP

If you are not sure if you have cut the right section or sections out, you could try producing a new clock chart with the reduced material so as to make sure that the presentation will still flow. If you become anxious about losing any material at all, even though the presentation flows in the new format, consider putting the extraneous material into a separate document for now. That way, you can work it up into a supporting handout if you want to later, perhaps for the Q & A session.

2. Rehearsal with script for timing only

For this run-through you might be happy to work from a script which has red pen all over it, with crossings out and additions throughout; for most presenters this is too much of a distraction. This is especially the case for this second rehearsal, when your principal concern is timing. For the sake of gaining an accurate timing, and remembering that you might need to make further amendments to the script, I would suggest that producing a fully revised script would be the best way forward.

You might surprise yourself in this rehearsal. Although you have only read through the material once, and have made additions and deletions since then, it may feel unexpectedly familiar: we are amazingly quick to pick up and retain language.

The work between the first and second rehearsal will have been vital: what you are hoping for here is a script which, when you read it aloud, makes sense, reads smoothly and makes your points effectively. If this is the case (and it usually will be) you are left considering only two things in this run-through: the strength of your argument and the timing of the presentation. If you find that either of these has gone drastically wrong, you will need to repeat the work you undertook after the first run-through, reworking both your plan and the script, but this is unlikely to be the case because of the work you have already undertaken. What is most likely here is that you will be tinkering with the script as you go, using your red pen this time to mark up places where you want to pause for effect, or where you can see that a new slide might begin, or a visual image might be useful. If you are a little over or under time there is no need to do anything about it at the moment; just remain aware of it as you go into the next part of the process.

Post-rehearsal activity

Prior to rehearsal number three you will need to move from a script (or, when you feel more confident as a presenter, a bullet-pointed series of notes, perhaps) to prompts. If you are, at this moment, feeling any reluctance to use prompts and instead would rather speak from a full script, let me quash that urge in you straight away. If you were giving a paper, you would be reading aloud from a written document; giving a presentation is quite a different thing. Reading from a script is rarely done well because if you are nervous, the pieces of paper shake loudly, if you are anxious, you can hide your entire face behind sheets of paper, and as you look down to read you are automatically pressing on your vocal chords, reducing your breathing capacity and losing eye contact, which inevitably means that you will speak faster, with less expression and no sense of contact with the audience. In a lecture this can work, because the audience is expecting this reduced level of interaction and variety; for a presentation it reduces your impact before you have even begun to try to get your point across.

Prompts come in several forms, so you can choose the one which works best for you:

- Prompt cards – sometimes referred to as index cards, these are postcard size (about 4" by 6") and so are prefect for holding discreetly in your hands as you go through your presentation. Presenters tend either to love or to hate prompt cards. They can feel more awkward than they ever look from the audience's perspective, and their presence can sometimes give a useful sense of occasion to a low key event. On the other hand, it might feel strange to you to be holding a set of cards from which to read, or you might forget to look down at them, leaving you lost when you finally remember to go back to them for reference. The only way to know is to try using them and see if they work for you.

- Prompt sheet – this is, in effect, a series of prompts on a piece of paper. These prompts might be just a list of the sections of your talk (in a large font, in bold) or they might be a series of text boxes about the size of a prompt cards, filled in with your prompt notes and spreading across several pages. If you use these, they should be taped to the table or lectern (or, at the least, held down by your watch or a pen) so that you are never tempted to pick them up: they are there only for you to glance at for reference every now and again.
- Slideshow prompt – this is a common enough technique, and can work extremely well. There are two potential pitfalls: if you put too much information on each slide, to remind yourself what to say, you might end up reading the slides (a maddening habit which you should avoid) or you will have such brief slides that they prompt you but are of little help to the audience.

Everyone finds their own way with presentation prompts. After many years I now tend to use a combination of data projector slides and a prompt sheet on the table. I make sure that the first slide shows my name and any other material relevant to the presentation (event, date, my position of expertise) and then the second slide would show the sections of my presentation. That way both the audience members and I can settle down, with all of us knowing where we are going. My other slides will sometimes be complicated, sometimes far more simple, but my prompt sheet reminds me of where I need to go next.

3. Rehearsal with prompts for content and timing

You have done a fair amount of 'behind the scenes' work up until this point in the preparation process. Although you have only read through the presentation twice, you have also planned and written a script, reduced that script down to make it more effective, then reduced the support even further by reducing your script to a series of prompts. From now on the process is a little more manageable; this run-through will be simply a case of you confirming as you go that your content now works nicely and checking at the end that the timing is correct. Remember that at the moment you have no presentation aids (such as a data projector slideshow) so you will still have to rehearse to a reduced time limit so as to allow for their inclusion later.

Post-rehearsal activity

You might have to make a few corrections, perhaps adding in an extra card or crossing out a small section on a card which now seems cumbersome, and you might be doing this in response either to your sense of how well your message is being conveyed or to the timing. If you discover that more extensive changes are needed you will have to go back a stage, but that is the beauty of a system like this: you can revert back and not lose track of what you are trying to achieve.

Although this stage is easier because there should be fewer alterations to the material, it can also be a little scary in prospect. You are no longer supported by a full script, so you will have to recall what it was you wanted to say and find the words at each moment to say it. In reality, it tends to be exhilarating. You have worked through this material twice already, so you will find the words you need, even if you stumble from time to time, and there will be a freshness and energy to your performance because you are now liberated from the script so you can look up and, perhaps for the first time, begin to focus fully on the audience which you can imagine to be in front of you as you rehearse.

 TOP TIP

If you trip over your words in this rehearsal it can be unnerving. Try, as much as you possibly can, to ignore this problem. It always feels awkward to the presenter when it happens, but audiences rarely notice it. I would expect to stumble over words every now and then in the final presentation. If I were working from a script this would leave me looking underprepared but as I would be talking naturally from my prompts, it would not have any negative impact upon the audience – we all stumble as we talk, from time to time; we just overlook it.

You need to be as brave as you can be with your prompts: the briefer the notes you make for yourself, the more natural will be the presentation. Here is an example of just how reduced prompt cards should ideally become.

Imagine that I have been asked to prepare a presentation of 20–25 minutes, to talk about a project that my organisation has agreed to undertake. I am to present with my colleague, Emma Bishop, and my role is to introduce the project and to field the questions at the end of the presentation.

The initial script might looks like this:

> For the last nine months our organisation has been preparing to undertake a major review of the environmental impact of continuing with the work to extend the M52 by 9.87km westwards to link Colemarket with Blackport.
>
> The scheme was first considered in 2010, but was dropped by the government of the time. Although they claimed that it was shelved as a result of environmental impact studies carried out in the previous year by Greenpeace North East Region, based in Newcastle, the study was never published. It has long been suspected that in fact finance was the stumbling block.
>
> We now have to go forward by reassessing the environmental situation. This is likely to include reviewing the original report (and deciding whether it

could have been influenced by any political bias), sourcing and analysing similar reports for the area from that time and undertaking our own major environmental impact review.

The problem that we face is one of timing. This initial stage must be completed within three months. Thereafter other teams will take over to carry out similar studies to assess the financial, political and transport implications of moving forward. We are here today to gain your support. We need commitment to the project, a willingness to work to a tight deadline, and an understanding that this is a politically and environmentally sensitive situation. It is going to be essential that we keep our work away from the prying eyes of the media until we reach a point when we feel ready to go public.

My colleague, Emma Bishop, whom many of you already know, will now outline for you the action that we need to take.

Whilst this script (which would be the opening part of a script produced after rehearsal number two) is effective in deciding what information to include in the presentation, I would lose impact if I just read it aloud. I would move it to prompt cards, reducing as I go, so that, after rehearsal number five, they would look like this:

Good morning – my name is Cindy Becker and I am going to be talking to you today with my colleague Emma Bishop, who most of you know.

25 mins

Q & A at the end

9 months	SLOW!!!
M52	
2010	**MAP**

Greenpeace North East Region

We now have to go forward:

Original report

Similar reports

TIMING – 3 MONTHS ONLY!!

KEEP IT QUIET!!

There are a few things to note from these prompt cards:

- They are significantly reduced from the original script.
- Although these could be index cards, they might also look like this, text boxes on a page which I have on the desk/lectern in front of me as I present. By using text boxes they still look like prompt cards and would remind me of the overall structure of my presentation so that I could pause for effect as I progress.
- I have included my full first sentence; if I am nervous I might forget this, even though the details would be on my first slide. What I want to avoid is just looking at the screen and reading it aloud; the audience can look at the screen whilst I glance at my prompts and then deliver a confident first sentence.
- The first card prompts me to remind the audience members of the structure of the event; that way, they can relax.
- On the left-hand side of the second card I have given very brief details of facts I need to recall; on the right-hand side are notes to remind me that I need to slow down (I talk too fast when I am nervous) and to nudge me to show a visual aid at this point – the map – because in rehearsals I kept forgetting to change to the next slide at this point. The map will then remind me of the details of the locations and distances.
- I think that I might forget that it is Greenpeace North East Region, so I have noted that on card three.
- Beyond that, I know that I could talk convincingly for the rest of the introduction, as long as I remind myself of the key points we need to get across.
- By keeping these notes so brief I will let the audience assimilate information from the screen but I will avoid talking from the screen.
- Note that the material used for this presentation is commercial and professional rather than research based; a useful reminder, I hope, that the skills you learn now will support you throughout your working life, wherever that leads you.

Each presenter finds his or her level when it comes to prompt cards and how much information to include. As long as your default position is to try to reduce the amount of material to a minimum, you will soon find the right level for you.

 EXERCISE

One way to practise producing perfect prompt cards, before you are preparing for a presentation and so tempted to include too much information, is to take a page of a book and produce text boxes as I did here, working on reducing a page of text to the briefest possible set of prompt card notes. Try producing them as the words come to you without too much thought, then reducing them to a more note-like state, then try presenting from them to see how little prompting you actually need in order to give an effective presentation.

4. Rehearsal with reduced prompts for visual aids

This is another important step in your progress towards an effective presentation. As you rehearse for the fourth time, keep in the back of your mind that your script cards will need to be reduced even more. Notice where you feel your prompt cards are too wordy. This is also the stage at which you will produce your visual aids, so as you run through think about where natural breaks might occur (this is where you move to a new data projector slide) and consider where you might introduce any other presentation material you plan to include, such as a demonstration, viewing an audio or film clip, or sharing web-page material with the audience.

Post-rehearsal activity

This might seem, at first consideration, to be rather late in the process to be producing your visual aids, but in fact this timing has advantages. It means that you will not have been tempted to produce a wordy script on a slide, so as to counter your nerves at the earlier stages of rehearsal, nor will you have wasted your time producing presentation support for material which you have since abandoned as unnecessary.

You have four potential sources of information for your presentation aids:

- You could simply start from scratch and rely on your memory of what you have just been presenting.
- Your full script, which hopefully you have not glanced at since rehearsal two, and so which you can now look at afresh to see if you could repeat information from here onto a visual aid.
- Your initial plan, which would help to remind you of your ultimate goal and the route to it as you prepare your visual aids.
- Your prompt cards, which may match nicely onto the slides you will produce.

You might have noticed that I referred here to 'information' rather than 'material'. This is because, whilst any of these might be useful in helping you decide what sort of presentation aid you want to use and what material will need to be shown in this way, none of them will have automatically given you the actual material itself. Cutting and pasting from your earlier script or from your prompts, or even from your plan, tends not to work terribly well: it can leave your presentation aids too cramped, or awkward, or looking and feeling too much like a 'mini-script'.

5. Rehearsal with prompts and aids for impact

You will surprise yourself now with how familiar your presentation material feels. You have prompts which work for you and presentation aids which will work well for the audience. This rehearsal will not see you stumbling over those visual aids, as you have produced them as an integral part of an already well-developed presentation, but it will give you an understanding of how well they add to the impact of the presentation, and that is really what your penultimate run through is all about.

Prior to this you were working to an under-length timing so as to accommodate your visual aids. Now you will rehearse as if to an audience, with full support. You will need to take time to allow your audience to read each slide as it appears, or to view your demonstration or to interact with the smartboard work you have prepared. If you are using web pages, go to them and allow time for the audience to absorb them as you work through this rehearsal. If you are using a film or audio clip, play it now so that you can confirm that its timing and placement achieves the greatest impact.

Post-rehearsal activity

There may be relatively little to do after this rehearsal, but it is a good chance to improve things in several ways:

- Make sure that all of the practical details are firm in your mind: the timing, the division between presenting and answering questions, the likely size of the audience, the technology available. That way, you can relax and focus on your final rehearsal.
- Look again at your prompt cards – could you achieve any final reduction in the amount of material on them?
- Think back to your presentation aids as you have just used them. Did each of them work as well as possible? Has every single one of your slides been checked for accuracy of spelling and other details?

Ideally, take a break before your final rehearsal. Free your mind from the process of preparing the presentation so that you can come refreshed to your next rehearsal; that way, you are far more likely to spot any last-minute glitches.

6. Final rehearsal for confidence

This run-through should be a pleasure. You will begin to feel a little more nervous, naturally: this is the end of preparing and so the event is nearly upon you. On the other hand, this is your final rehearsal and you have worked hard. You are familiar with the material and can feel confident that you can convey your message. You have considered the questions you might be asked and you have ensured that there is a logical flow through your presentation, which is well supported by your presentation aids. The timing should work well and you can feel pleased with yourself.

 TOP TIP

Try not to undermine yourself in this final rehearsal. It is supposed to be giving you a confidence boost before you present, but if you become anxious and start altering your slides or other visual aids, or decide to change the order of your points for no reason except that you are nervous, you will be working against yourself. Your focus needs to be on presenting what you have to the absolute best of your ability, not changing the presentation.

A note on the timing: by now it will have increased, with the inclusion of your visual aids, to about 17–18 minutes for every 20 minutes of presentation time you have been given. This may seem illogical, given that you might naturally assume that you want to use every possible minute you have been given so as to include as much material and argument as you can. However, this is to overlook the reality of presenting. A presentation usually takes a little longer than you would expect, because whoever is introducing you will take a few moments longer than you had anticipated, then you smile at the delegates and stand silent for a while waiting for them to smile back, then you ad lib unexpectedly every now and then, or you find that the audience is clearly taking longer to read through your slides than you took to skim through them in rehearsal. Also, with the pressure of performance, you will find a gravitas and sense of occasion which was lacking in rehearsal and so you speak just a little more slowly and with just a touch more emphasis. All of this takes time, so leaving yourself that amount of space in your timing makes sense.

Post-rehearsal activity

Nothing. Nothing at all. Do not give in to the pressure to 'just run through it' six more times, or succumb to the nagging feeling that you might get from time to time that it needs a little more tweaking. Instead, remember how calm and resolved you felt about giving the presentation at the end of your final rehearsal; that is the feeling you need to be able to recall as the event comes closer.

The only exception to this general rule of leaving well alone is if you have prepared your paper or presentation several weeks before the event. In that case it might be useful to recapture the content before you actually present, but I would still urge you to avoid a full series of rehearsals at the last minute, which might make you more nervous or inclined to change your material. Instead, read through the paper or presentation under your breath and sitting down, so that it is a low-key rendition of what you are about to achieve. It will be enough.

 TOP TIP

Although some presenters find it valuable to film their rehearsals so as to gauge the impact of what they are trying to do, I would be cautious about this. Unless you are very familiar with, and happy about, the way you look on film, it is easy to focus too much on your minor mannerisms and slight stumbling (which the audience will not notice), or to be reminded that you have never much liked your nose. Films can rob you of confidence, so try filming yourself just carrying out an everyday activity well in advance of practising for a presentation. See how you respond to that film before making the decision to film your presentation rehearsals.

If a paper or presentation is well prepared and delivered thoughtfully by a presenter who has clearly rehearsed and is keen to get a message across, then it will succeed in much of what the presenter has set out to do. With experience that presenter will be able to present with greater assurance and will acquire a higher level of skill in this area. That is what the next chapter is about: increasing the impact of your event by eliminating presenting problems and deliberately employing techniques which work.

Ten

DELIVERING YOUR MATERIAL

My intention in the last chapter was to offer you a process by which you could deliver a workable presentation, a step-by-step system which you could work through as you prepare to present. This chapter is a little different. Even if you read it through several times, you would not be able to put all of its points into practice straight away. Presenting with impact is a cumulative process, one which you will develop over time, so as we go through this chapter you could pick out just one or two things at a time, get into the habit of presenting with those techniques, and then return here again once they are mastered, ready to try out the next technique. You will know where your greatest presentation anxiety lies, so once you have read through the chapter you might return first to the section which you believe will be of most immediate help to you.

Using your voice

It will probably come as no surprise to you to see that I have chosen this as the first, and most important, aspect of presentation technique. If you accept that you are more important than any presentation aids you introduce, and also that your voice is the instrument you need to tune in order to give a pleasing rendition of your material, then you will agree with me that the voice is the place to start. I will work through various aspects of your vocal performance, highlighting what can go wrong and suggesting how you can improve.

Too loud: I have begun with this potential problem because it is rare and so you can probably ignore it as a possibility entirely. There are just a few people who, when nervous, react by speaking too loudly. Ask a friend or colleague who has been with you in a professional or social situation in which you were nervous; if you did not speak too loudly then, you are most unlikely to speak too loudly during a presentation.

If you do have a natural tendency to talk a little too loudly when you are anxious, ask a supporter to sit in the audience for your next few presentations and give you a discreet signal if you talk too loudly, but only if you are too loud after a few minutes. You may have experienced the effect of 'initial loudness' in a theatre. When the curtain goes up and the play begins, it can seem as if the actors are all speaking in an unnatural way, being far too enunciated and loud. Over the course of a few minutes two things happen: the audience become accustomed to the slightly louder than normal speech at the same time as the actors calm down and moderate their voices to the space. After this, loudness is not an issue for anyone; as this is also the case in presentations, give yourself a minute or so before you begin to worry.

Too soft: A voice which is too soft is a far more common problem, and is not restricted to those who have a naturally soft speaking voice. The issue is caused by nerves and so is usually fixed by conquering and then using your nerves (more of this in the next chapter). Projecting your voice, as an actor would do, takes much work and can lead to the unnatural projection and volume I have just mentioned. Instead, there is an easier way to increase the impact of your voice. If you work on the voice exercises given here, and go through the breathing exercise in the next chapter, you will be able to take greater control of your voice.

 EXERCISE

Do these exercises in order, in one go, both as an aid in the days leading up to a presentation and as a regular part of your life if you are planning to present (or act, or teach, or preach) regularly.

1 Stand somewhere where you are happy to shout out loud and where nobody is watching so that you will not feel restricted in any way.

2 Stand straight, with your chin up and your shoulders back. This might feel a little awkward at first, but that is fine; do not go so far as to feel any discomfort, though. Sitting down and/ or looking down will always subdue your voice. If you are expected to sit as you present be aware of this problem. For the purposes of this exercise, stay standing throughout.

3 Pretend that you have a very chewy sweet or tough piece of food in your mouth and move your jaw muscles as if you were chewing very determinedly. If you are tense or have not spoken to anyone for a few hours this might feel a little uncomfortable; you might even hear your jaw crack or crackle, but this is normal. Especially for those people who grind their

teeth in their sleep or tense their jaw when they concentrate, this part of the process is important for opening up the potential of your jaw and mouth.

4   Having worked your jaw, you need to focus it and ensure that your jaw, tongue and vocal chords are working at their hardest and best. Without in any way trying to raise or lower the volume of your voice, say, slowly and repeatedly 'thick, black, dark, clean chocolate beans'. As you repeat, really work your mouth – be conscious of the shape it is making and get every bit of expression you can out of the words, especially 'beans' – you should feel your lips elongating as the sentence ends.

5   Now hum very gently, just to get used to the sound of you voice in your head. By humming you are focusing on tone, timbre and volume, not words: this gives you a better instinctive insight into what your voice is doing.

6   Now lay your hand flat on your diaphragm and press, *gently*. You can find this huge muscle fairly easily: it sits at the base of your ribs, just below your solar plexus. You will know when your hand is in the right place because when you resume humming, you will find that the volume naturally increases as you press, and subsides again when you remove your hand.

7   You will now have an idea of the volume and feel of the natural state of your 'resting' voice (your first piece of humming) and your 'exerted voice' (as you pressed gently on your diaphragm) – you are ready to make your voice work for you.

8   Imagine that you have just received amazingly good news: clench your fists, punch the air, jump up and down – do whatever you would do if you really had received splendiferous news. Alongside these actions, shout 'yes!' with enthusiasm. Do this several times to release your voice, observing how your face and mouth feel and how good it sounds just to shout out loud like this.

9   As you do this, you may be struck by the fact that we rarely shout in any public place; indeed, many of us avoid shouting anywhere. There is a theory that public sporting events are so popular at least in part because they give us permission to shout, loudly and collectively. Now that you have shouted out a few times, bring together all of the work you have done by shouting, firmly and loudly, 'crash, bang, wallop'. Force yourself to increase the volume without losing the quality; you do not want to end up raising the pitch so that you are screeching; you want an assertive, powerful voice.

10   Lastly, bring your voice back down to its natural resting state by humming again. You may find that you are humming rather loudly or with too much variation at first after your voice exertions, but keep going until you are humming at a moderate, steady rate.

Now that you have introduced yourself to the control you have over your voice, and the power you can generate, it is time to transfer this to the space in which you will be presenting. If it is not possible to work in the actual space in which you will present, try to find a room which is similar in size and layout. Furniture tends to muffle sound, whilst a lecture theatre can amplify certain sounds strangely, so the layout is as important as the size. If you cannot find anything suitable, at least move into a public room of some sort so that you can gain a sense of how your voice sounds in a public space.

If the situation allows, you could carry out these exercises all over again in that public space. If this is not possible, carry out the breathing and relaxation techniques that I will be discussing with you in the next chapter and simply give your paper or rehearse your presentation in the space. You will not necessarily need to work through it in its entirety, but run through enough to make you feel more comfortable hearing your voice in the space. Have someone sitting at the back of the space so that your voice level is monitored. This supporter will need to be ready to signal to you if your voice dips, and must also be prepared to move around the space from time to time to make sure that your voice carries to all parts. On the day of the presentation, if a supporter can sit at the back and smile encouragingly if your voice level is right, so much the better.

Accents: if you are concerned that you have an especially strong regional or national accent, and that people will struggle to understand what you are saying as a result, make sure that this really is a problem before you work on it. We often assume that we have a problem in this area where actually none exists. Elocution training to redress this problem can be expensive and time consuming, so instead of rushing to this option, think about how you can work with the voice you have.

Presentations and papers are such pleasurable occasions because there is a real person standing up in front of us talking. It is not a film, or a slide-show which we were sent in the post, or a document through which we have to wade in order to understand the points: someone has taken the time and trouble to prepare an event especially for us, and is now standing in front of us delivering the paper or presentation. As audience members we are a little relieved that it is not us standing up there, we have an interest in the area being considered and we want to engage with the propositions being offered to us. If we cannot hear every single word, crystal clear and with no hesitation, just because the speaker's accent differs from the speech we usually hear, we will not worry about it. Instead, we will keep a close eye on the presentation slides to make sure that we keep up and we will enjoy the bits we can hear clearly (which will rapidly increase in number as we get used to the speaker's voice).

So, to some extent, even an apparent problem is not necessarily as big a problem as you might at first assume. However, you will naturally want to reduce the challenge to the audience as much as possible so that attention remains firmly on what you have to say rather than on how it is being said. The answer lies not just in having perhaps a greater number of visual aids than you would otherwise produce, to ensure that nobody gets lost, but also in a voice trick that can work very well.

Slowing down might not work in this situation because it results, in those places where your accent is not affecting intelligibility, in your audience finding your delivery ponderous and unexciting. The secret is to introduce tiny little pauses every now and then. These will not change your accent at all, but they will allow audience members to catch up with what you are saying, without them having had any particular feeling of ever having been behind. It is a trick which requires practice: pauses which are too frequent, too long or badly placed will leave the audience confused. Generally, a tiny little pause at the end of every third sentence or so works well. The best way to master the technique is to practise it repeatedly, not forcing the pauses but allowing them to drop in whenever it feels most natural to the sense of what you are trying to say, with a supporter looking on who can tell you if you are succeeding in becoming clearer in your speech without it sounding too artificial.

Enunciation and word slur: the effect of this problem, and the solutions, are similar to the issues which arise from a regional or national accent. If you tend to slur words together it might not matter for most of your presentation, but work through it (with a supportive listener if possible) to see whether there are any words that will cause a problem. A missing 't' sound is the most common of these. I come from Berkshire in England, where missing 't' sounds are endemic in the local style of speech. I am used to 'compu'er' for 'computer' and 'wa'er' for 'water'. This sound is actually quite easy to recall and insert once you are in a formal setting and so remember to do it, but if you struggle with this, or whichever other letter sounds you miss out, or words that you tend to slur together, the solution is similar to that for accents: a tiny pause between words that would cause problems if they are run together or, if your enunciation is a more significant problem, little pauses after every few sentences. If you are talking about figures (did you say '14 nodes' or 40 nodes'?) then it is also perfectly acceptable to repeat the phrase, slowly, for both clarity and emphasis.

Too many words: if you run out of breath during a paper or presentation, this could have several effects on you and your presentation style. You might sound a little breathless, you might inserts pauses in unnatural places in your sentences, or you could feel a little light headed. There are two reasons why this happens, and both are easy to fix. The first could be that you are speaking too much from a script which is in written rather than spoken language. This means that your prompts have not been reduced enough and so are like 'mini-scripts' rather than true prompts. If this is not the case it is probable that you are struggling to maintain a good rhythm of breathing; I will be working though breathing techniques with you in the next chapter.

Stammering: the decision you need to make, if you stammer when you give a paper or presentation, is how distracting you and the audience are likely to find it. These reactions are linked: generally, a speaker with a slight stammer who is aware of it and simply ignores it is giving a strong cue to the audience, which also ignores it. After a surprisingly short amount of time nobody in the room is even thinking about the stammer; the focus is where it needs to be: on the material.

However, if you have a stammer which makes it difficult for you to speak in public, you might want to do some work on it. This could be a lengthy process, so be prepared to begin early and dedicate time and effort to it. I once knew a presenter who had a severe stammer and decided that, rather than working on his stammer, he would adapt his presentations. He produced the most amazing visual effects: perfect data projector slides which were designed to demonstrate stages in a process by the layering of text, interspersed with films of him demonstrating his work and talking about it to camera (when, interestingly, he never stammered). The reason these worked so well was that, whilst they reduced to an absolute minimum what he was required to say during the presentation, his facial expressions and enthusiastic, smiling demeanour as he showed his presentation aids left the audience in no doubt as to his passion for his subject and his dedication to sharing his research. I think this proves that we can all find our own way to achieve our goals.

Using your language

Your own language: I have tended to assume in this guide that you will be speaking in 'your language' but I recognise that you might be speaking in your second (or third, or fourth) language, so some tips on this first.

Giving an interpreted talk is part of this language challenge. If you are speaking, for example, in sign language, you will be familiar with this method of communication and, unless the talk is being voice glossed, you will naturally leave appropriate pauses for the interpreter to voice-over. If your talk is being simultaneously interpreted from your spoken language to another, you can rely on the professional interpreter to do most of the hard work for you, although you might want to spend a few minutes (if time allows) to work together before the event. The problem of interpretation is one reason why you might be asked to deliver a paper rather than having the freedom of a presentation, where your ad libs and deviation from the plan could cause problems. This way, the interpreter can simply deliver your talk as you do, from the prepared script.

If your words are not being interpreted because you are able to deliver your presentation in a language which is not your first, you obviously need to ensure that you can be understood in this public setting. I stress the public nature of the event here, because it is common for people to be well understood amongst a group of friends in informal settings, whereas on a stage with a distance between speaker and audience, the language barrier becomes more noticeable.

If you are not sure about how clearly you would come across in this setting, practise in front of a small group of supporters who are sitting across the depth and width of a presentation room to replicate as nearly as possible the experience of speaking publically. If this seems to work well, you will give your paper or presentation with some confidence, but arrange to have a supporter in the audience who will tell you how easy you were to understand on the day. If there were problems of the audience understanding your words, use the techniques I have suggested around accents to help you improve the impact of your presentations in future.

Written versus spoken language: although I have already mentioned the problems associated with working from a full script, it is worth noting here that some speakers also tend to fall into this style of speech whenever they are nervous. Of course you will want to sound formal and professional, but if you would not normally use words and phrases such as 'persons', 'furthermore', 'notwithstanding', 'in conclusion' and so forth, try to avoid them when you present your research. I should point out that I happily use 'furthermore' and 'notwithstanding' in my day-to-day speech, as do many people (although 'persons' is ridiculous, in my view). There is no definitive list of words which are always either 'spoken' or 'written' English, and of course any research activity is likely to introduce new words into your vocabulary; the rule is to avoid using too many words which you would never use in natural speech, on the basis that they will feel strange to you and so could have a negative impact on your presentation style.

Formal language: even though you will want to avoid using too many words which sound strange or unfamiliar to you, you will not want to lose your formality. This means asking a supporter to watch one of your rehearsals, listening out for any use of language which makes you sound too casual and not impressive enough. You would be surprised at how many people swear or blaspheme, for example, with no idea that they are doing it. Be aware and take precautions to ensure that this is not you.

Addictive language: this is hugely irritating, for speaker and audience alike, particularly as it is so difficult to eradicate. Imagine for a moment that you have a personal tic which comes up again and again in your speech. It will usually be a cliché of some sort and will never add anything to the meaning of your sentence. It will not usually be more than four to five words long. I would include in this category single words such as 'like', 'basically' and 'so', slightly longer phrases such as 'you know', 'as it were' 'to be honest', 'for sure' and 'it is obvious', and also quite cumbersome phrases such as 'in point of fact', 'at the end of the day' and 'at this moment in time'.

The problem is that, once you start to use them, these tics are addictive: it is difficult to think of any way to say the sentence which does not include your favourite word or phrase, except, of course, we are not usually thinking at all when we employ these words – we simply use them without any conscious effort. As with many other aspects of presenting being considered in this chapter, you are likely to need outside help on this. First, ask friends and family if they have noticed that you have a favourite word or phrase which you use repeatedly. Then ask a supporter to listen to one of your rehearsals with that verbal tic in mind, but also with an awareness that other redundant words and phrases might have crept into your language. Once they are pointed out to you, it takes no more than a little effort to eradicate them, even when you are nervous.

Tone: for some scholars, the move from normal conversation to a formal presentation is no more than a small jump, because some of us naturally talk in a formal, considered manner. For others of us, the move is more difficult. This is sometimes because a speaker naturally talks in a very casual style and so struggles to talk in a more serious way. If you are overly anxious, your attempts to be an enthusiastic and friendly speaker can come across as flippant, almost offhand. For others, taking their work seriously can make them appear severe, almost cross with an audience. This is also exacerbated by nervousness. These problems can be entrenched behaviour, partly because you might not have noticed how your manner and tone of voice changes in this situation.

Once again, ask a supporter about this and, once you are aware of a problem, you can work through it in rehearsals to eliminate any infelicitous tone of voice or style of presenting. If you want to bring out this type of errant manner so that you can work on ridding yourself of it, it can help if one of your final rehearsals takes place in circumstances as near to the reality of the final event as you can make them. Rehearse in a space similar to the event location, invite a number of supporters along, do not allow yourself to deviate from what you are trying to do by any interruptions, but rather give your paper or presentation as you would on the day. This might induce the nervousness which will bring out the voice tone or attitude which you will display for the talk itself.

A note about humour. If you are naturally amusing, you might be tempted to inject some humour but this is extremely difficult to do well on stage. A joke could fall flat, and even if it is a good joke the audience might be made so anxious by the very fact of a joke that it is unable to respond appropriately. It is worth noticing, however, that audience members, perhaps because they are relieved that the speaker is confident and they feel so much goodwill towards someone whose work is interesting them, are really rather disposed to smile – even to laugh. You can turn this to your advantage. Jokes or other scripted and extended attempts at humour are difficult to inject into a formal presentation or paper, but the odd aside can work well, as long as you are sharing an experience common to the audience and you avoid any chance of offence. So, for example, 'Working this research through the ethics committee – a delightfully simple task, as we all know …', with a lift of your eyebrows, will only raise a smile or laugh amongst members of the audience who have experienced the rigours of an ethics committee proce-dure and, of course, if there are not dedicated and/or opinionated members of an ethics committee in the room. The rule with humour is to keep it light and natural and, if you have any doubts at all, leave it well alone.

The pace of delivery

Just as it is rare for a speaker to talk too loudly, so too is it unusual for pre-senters to talk too slowly. If you suspect that this might be the case for you, it would be a good idea to ask a supporter to check this for you the next time you speak in public, but it is more likely that you are simply getting used to your 'presentation voice'. This is a slower voice than any of us would use in our everyday conversations; if the pace of your speech as you present feels a little odd and slow to you, you probably have it about right.

Of course, the audience never notices that you are talking a little more slowly than you would do if you were chatting to any member of the audi-ence individually, but you will notice and it is important that you keep noticing so that you avoid speeding up as the talk continues. For more inexperienced speakers (and also for some far more experienced speakers, it should be admitted), they begin a little too fast and then they slow down to a good presenting speed as they settle into the occasion.

 TOP TIP

Some speakers deliberately induce a feeling of unfamiliarity in their presentation situation so that they are reminded, almost without being aware of this, that the occasion is formal and the pace of their voice needs to be appropriately slow. Some take their watch off and place it in front of them, even though they might never check the time; others wear more formal clothing or higher heels; I tend to wear my long hair up, because I would never do this for a casual event. Anything which reminds you of the sense of occasion can help to slow your voice.

Having established that you might speak too fast, it would be useful for you to test the speed of you voice, so that you can learn how you need to change your natural pace and also so that you get a sense of how it feels to speak at a pace which suits a presentation.

 EXERCISE

I have written the paragraph below in a spoken style of language and it contains 156 words, which would take roughly a minute to deliver at a sensible presentation speed. I say 'roughly' because your style of speaking might lend itself to a slight faster or marginally slower speed of delivery. Try reading it aloud now, timing yourself as you go:

> It is often the case that we do not give a moment's thought to the speed of our speech. We don't really need to: the person to whom we are speaking is likely to be near to us, to have the benefit of seeing our natural body language, and to understand exactly the context within which we are speaking. Once you stand up to give a presentation, this situation changes entirely. The members of your audience may not know you, or even know much about the subject on which you are about to present. You can assume that they will be reasonably interested, but it is up to you to maintain and, if possible, enhance that interest. The speed of your speech is vital to this endeavour: too fast and they will lose your point entirely, too slow and they will soon get bored. It is a tricky thing to master, but well worth the effort.

You would have been speaking a little slower than normal as you read this because you knew that it is an exercise on speech pace and you are not especially nervous, but your timing will give you an idea of the amount of work you have to do in altering your pace. For your second rehearsal, whilst you are still working to a fairly full script, ask a supporter to time a section of your talk so that you can check your words per minute once the rehearsal is over. If you are working from a bullet-pointed set of notes rather than a full script, try reading this exercise through three times in a row to the correct time before a rehearsal, to remind you of the pace of speech needed for your paper or presentation.

 TOP TIP

If you know that you tend to talk too quickly at the outset of a public appearance, try including some interesting but inessential information in the first minutes. This might include, for example, basic information about you and your presentation which is also shown on a data projector slide. This has the dual advantage of allowing the delegates the chance to read what they cannot easily hear and also slowing you down because you are showing a slide rather than just talking.

Silence in your presentation

It may be unexpected, after so much work on your words and your voice, to ask you to consider with me the use of silence in your presentation. However, to overlook silence would be to miss the opportunity to add significantly to the impact of your event.

 CHECKLIST

There are many moments in which you might include silence in your presentation or when giving a paper, some of which will come more naturally than others:

- at the beginning of your presentation;
- as you change the visual aid;
- when you finish one aspect of your subject;
- in a natural away, to give emphasis;
- before and after a vital phrase or fact;
- before and after figures, names and references;
- as you finish your talk.

At the beginning of your presentation: this is the most difficult silence, both to initiate and maintain. However much easier it is to rush straight in, you need to be still and silent, making eye contact with the audience and waiting until the general hubbub dies down. If you are being introduced by a chairperson you will not have this problem, but still a smile and a few moments' silence just after you have thanked the chairperson for the glowing introduction and just before you speak adds a sense of expectation to the occasion.

 TOP TIP

Please remember that this is not a power play, nor a re-enactment of a schoolroom drama. Do not stand in expectant silence until every single member of the audience is absolutely quiet before you will deign to break silence and utter your first word. As you can probably tell from my tone, this tactic is guaranteed to breed resentment in the audience.

As you move to the next presentation aid: it would be counter-productive to try to give you a precise time to allow for an audience to absorb the information on a single data projector slide, or to look through a page of a handout. Instead, ensure that you get the timing right by looking at the presentation aid along with the audience, briskly reading through it or looking at every image yourself, then turn back to the audience. When the majority of faces are turned back to you, begin to speak again.

 TOP TIP

Audience members often feel that they need permission to look away from you. By looking at the presentation aid alongside the audience members you are not only gauging the time it will take them to absorb the information, you are also breaking eye contact and so making it easier for them to look at the aid.

When you finish one aspect of your subject: an audience needs auditory clues as to what is happening, as well as visual cues which they receive from a change in slide or the start of a film, audio clip or demonstration. You can offer instruction, such as asking audience members to look at the next page of a handout, but if nothing is going to change visually and there is nothing new for them to do, signal the move by a moment of silence before you move on to the next area of your paper or presentation.

In a natural away, to give emphasis: we usually think that we give emphasis to a phrase or word in two ways: by making our voice louder, or by repetition. We tend to overlook the third way: we also pause, often both before and after the word or phrase. So, we might say (with // representing a pause) 'We now know that // more than *ninety* per cent // of the world's bee population is under threat'. We would naturally stress 'more than *ninety* per cent' by raising our voice a little; if we feel very strongly we might raise our voice even more on the word 'ninety'. If we felt that this was the key point of our speech we might say 'We now know that // more than *ninety* per cent, // that is // *ninety per cent,* // of the world's bee population is under threat'. If you say this aloud to yourself now, giving it due emphasis, you will also notice that you leave a minuscule pause before the word 'more' the first time it is used, and you will also leave a similar pause after the words 'per cent'. In the sentence with the repeated phrase you would also repeat these pauses.

Although you do this naturally on occasion, it helps to do it more deliberately in a paper or presentation and to include practising the pauses as part of each of your rehearsals. At the end of each run through ask yourself whether you remembered to include some deliberate pauses for emphasis.

Before and after a vital phrase or fact: sometimes you will want an audience to know that a point is vital, but you do not want to make it seem controversial, or sound as if you are being argumentative, by raising the volume of your voice. A pause allows you to get this message across. Small pauses, for example, just before and straight after the sentence 'This is not a matter for government' makes it clear that you will brook no argument on this issue: it is a given and you intend to move on firmly, on the basis that everyone agrees the point.

Before and after figures, names and references: audiences are not always adept at picking up on every fact and figure being offered. Although you may be able to confirm these on a visual presentation aid of some sort, it also helps if you pause fractionally before you give the information. This is particularly the case if figures could be confused ('40' for '14', for example, as I suggested earlier).

As you finish your talk: the seconds between finishing your talk and receiving the first question necessarily generate some silence. Even the most eager audience members will take a little time to gather their wits and formulate their query into a question in their minds before asking it. I will be talking to you about questions and answers in more detail later in this book, but for now it is sufficient to ask you to recognise this pause; it is an important one and must be respected, however awkward you feel as you wait for your first questioner.

People have often come to me to tell me that they have a problem with some aspect of presenting. They are convinced that they move their hands about too much, or that they stumble over their words, or that they do not have a commanding stage presence. More often than you would expect they are wrong in their diagnosis of the problem – they are simply not letting enough silence happen. It is one of the most powerful tools you have in a presentation and learning to harness it will be instrumental in your success.

Your stance as you present

If you are seated and giving a paper to a group you might not need to give much thought to how you appear. You will have dressed appropriately and you will try not to fiddle with your hair or fidget with a pen as you talk, but beyond that you are free simply to give your paper. If you are standing to give a paper or a presentation then things are naturally a little more complicated. You will want to appear calm and in control, and the relaxation and breathing techniques in this guide will help you to achieve this, but you can also work on how you actually look as you present.

The key here, funnily enough, is your toes. They should be facing the audience for most of your event and they should be just a little bit wider apart than your hips. Make sure that you are not taking your weight on just one of your hips – this always looks too casual – and glance down at your toes every now and then to see what they are doing. It sounds strange, I know, but speakers are often so caught up in the event that they fail to notice that they are prancing around the stage, or standing absolutely still and rigid. Your toes should not be in the same position throughout your presentation, but neither should they be dancing about. If you turn to face the screen or some other presentation aid, make sure that when you are ready to face the members of the audience again, your toes are pointing towards them; it feels very clumsy if the rest of your body does not follow, so you can be sure that you will not end up talking to the screen rather than the audience.

 TOP TIP

Probably the single most common problem with presenting, aside from speaking too fast, is 'hiding' from the audience. There are several ways you might do this but the two most popular are avoided by a consideration of your toes. Presenters tend either to look at the screen as a new slide appears and then 'forget' to look back at the audience properly, or they stand right in front of the screen, as if forgetting that it is there, or hoping that the image on the screen is somehow hiding them. If you are liable to either of these tendencies, keep your toes facing the audience when you are speaking and keep them well away from the area of the screen.

Non-verbal communication

Also referred to as body language, or shortened to NVC, this is a huge topic and one that could take several books to explore. Luckily, you do not have to be an expert in this area in order to make NVC work for you as you present. All you need do is learn to read some basic signals in your audience. Your own body language challenges will be relatively few and will either be covered here or explored in the next chapter.

 CHECKLIST

The most common NVC you need to recognise in an audience are indicators of these conditions:

• defensive;
• dominant;

(Continued)

(Continued)

- angry;
- deceptive;
- aggressive;
- invasive;
- bored;
- unwell;
- enthusiastic.

As we think through each of these postures, try to recall events where you have seen them in action, or people who tend to display them.

Defensive: a classic pose from listeners who feel threatened, intellectually or professionally, by what you are saying. It involves crossing the arms, with the chin lowered as if almost tucked in and an unwillingness to make eye contact. If the furniture allows, this pose also involves twisting legs at the ankle so that they begin to encircle a chair leg. This is the listener who will either say nothing in the Q & A session or who could surprise you by asking an abrupt, possibly aggressive question.

I have begun with this pose for two reasons: first, this is, in my view, the most dangerous type of listener because the pose can look deceptively quiet, almost meek, until the Q & A session. Second, it is the one pose which can be adopted relatively easily by the speaker if the occasion is such that the speakers remain seated. I have a friend and colleague with whom I have very much enjoyed teaching in the past, but I was always fascinated by the way he could deliver an entire session sitting down in this pose. He even found it difficult at times to write on the board because he had to untangle his legs from the chair and unbend his arm to reach out for a pen, yet he never noticed that he was doing it.

Dominant: this attitude comes second in this list because it can look deceptively similar to the defensive pose. The arms are still crossed, but this time the chin is jutting up and, if space allows, the listener might have legs stretched out a little in front. The body language is open and seems relaxed: this is someone effectively showing you their whole body, knowing that as the dominant party you will do nothing to attack it.

What you do, if anything, about this listener will depend on who it is. If a supporter, then this stance is simply protective of your position; if a powerful person in an organisation this posture might have become second nature and mean nothing at all in this circumstance; if a stranger, be ready for any type of question but if it is difficult for you to give a full and accurate answer straight away, offer to contact that person after the event rather than trying to bluff your way through or engage in a lengthy debate.

Angry: you will know this stance – we all do – and it differs relatively little between a colleague in heated debate, a sulking combatant after an argument, or an angry audience member. The listener will lean forward a little, often with hands on knees if space allows, with a frown on the face and determined eye contact. It is the eye contact you will probably notice first because it will be so prolonged, perhaps even becoming a stare. This is not a comfortable listener to have noticed, but luckily the question which might result from this anger is likely to be ill thought through and unfocused and, being calmer, you will be able to handle it easily enough.

Deceptive: listeners and speakers can fall into this attitude under stress. It involves repetitive and unexpected fiddling (stroking your nose, pulling on an ear lobe, playing with a pen whilst you repeatedly glance at it) or gestures which allow you to hide (putting your hand up over your face in order to sweep back your hair, rubbing between your eyebrows with your whole hand thus covering your face). Eye contact will be sporadic and will tend to slope across (and sometimes up) to one side.

Seeing this type of NVC in a listener could be useful to you: you are in a powerful position in that you are not trying to hide anything and so will be able to strengthen the force of your argument through your more straightforward NVC as you respond to this questioner. One word of caution: this is stressed behaviour, and so should be studiously avoided by the presenter who might have nothing to hide and yet display this NVC simply in reaction to stress.

Aggressive: although you might expect this NVC to look the same as the angry listener, and this can be the case, it might be that the stance is quite different. The angry listener is easy to counter in a Q & A session whilst the aggressive listener is likely to be more persistent and will also, perhaps, try to turn the audience from you, so look out for the differences. The aggressive listener might seem ill disposed to engage with you at all, rather ostentatiously looking away from you, perhaps out of the window, for most of your talk. There might be crossed legs, and there will certainly be movement: swaying feet, the repeated clicking of a pen, or the rustling of papers. There might even, with this listener, be sound. Whilst the angry listener might tut out loud and frown at certain points, the aggressive listener is more likely to sigh every now and then, just to let you know that the material is open to question, or rather a disappointment. As you can see, this type of listener is not easy as an audience member, let alone a questioner.

Invasive: you will sometimes have been in the presence of a speaker who makes you feel uncomfortable by leaning forward a little too far, or moving away from the screen and too far towards the audience. Whilst speakers can invade space, invasive listeners tend to invade material. They might occasionally lean forward too far if they are in the front row, or sit with their side very obviously facing you, but they are more likely to be rifling unnecessarily through the paperwork you have provided, sometimes sighing as if you have been unclear as to which portion of the material is relevant to this section of your talk.

The main difficulty with this type of NVC is that the solution seems temptingly simple: you can just ask the listener if you are being clear enough, or if the instructions make sense, or if help is needed in confirming a point or elaborating upon it. The invasive listener will often assure you at this point that there is no problem at all, and might even seem surprised that you are asking, before returning to exactly the same behaviour within moments. However hard it is, try to ignore this NVC; luckily, this type of listener is often silent when it comes to Q & A.

Bored: it is highly unlikely that you will be lucky enough to avoid bored listeners for your whole career as a presenter. They will not be resolutely refusing to make eye contact, but it might happen because they are busy with their phone or doodling on the handout in front of them. They will look up and might not seem to notice that you are talking at all; if they do they will smile at you but with only the vaguest sense of what you are saying. They might fiddle or fidget but this will not be deliberate or rhythmic, but rather an unconscious by-product of their boredom. If you produce some spectacularly arresting material or presentation aid they might look up and catch your eye, but beyond that you do not need to take them into account.

Notice that I mentioned luck in the last paragraph. That is because this NVC is highly unlikely to be anything to do with you. This listener might have signed up to four similar sessions in a row without realising it, or the order of presentations has been altered and you are now in a row of three, with each presenter using similar presentation aids, or maybe the lunch was especially good. It could be, perhaps, that this listener has only the most passing interest in your material and came along to the event to support a friend, or it might be the case that some of your listeners signed up for a session before yours whose title was misleading and whose content was very similar to yours. Fortunately, you will only find a small minority (sometimes of one) of bored listeners at any presentation, so you can happily overlook their presence, except to smile if you happen to catch their eye.

Unwell: I have included this type of listener just as a reminder that sometimes body language can mean nothing at all in relation to your talk. A listener who has a headache might sigh, put a hand across the face and sit awkwardly; a person who is hard of hearing might lean forward, whilst someone who has a bad back might assume a string of awkward positions as the talk progresses, even to the point of standing up at times, yet these same listeners might be your greatest supporters. You cannot afford to ignore body language, but nor must you become so convinced of its meaning that you overlook the possibility that it might have nothing to do with you or your presentation.

You might also be starting to feel as if your next presentation will see you faced with a front row full of the socially inept, all of whom will be gesturing madly and posturing wildly; this will not be the case, of course. Most people simply sit and listen attentively, thank goodness.

Enthusiastic: as with anger, we all know how this looks, from the way our friends respond when we give them our good news, to the postures our family adopt at celebrations, to the way people tend to look when they are watching a good show or an exciting film. The point here is not to recognise the NVC – that will be easy – but to harness the power of mirroring. Although the mirroring effect of NVC is sometimes exaggerated by those who are convinced of the power of this type of analysis, it is certainly the case that if you cross your legs whilst you talk to a group, some of them are likely to cross their legs too (this is quite good fun to try out on a crowded train).

Inducing a bout of leg crossing is not very useful to you as a presenter, perhaps, but if you apply the principle to smiling, with an open-faced enthusiasm, perhaps with eyes wide when you want to emphasise a particularly exciting or surprising point, you will find that some of your audience members will follow your lead and will feel even keener on what you are saying as a result.

There is good reason why I have not suggested in this section that you need to work too hard on your own NVC, beyond the common problems tackled in the next chapter. Here I have been showing you how NVC might possibly reveal the inner emotions of audience members, effectively how their body might betray them. If your NVC reflected your inner emotions at the outset of a presentation it might not be a good thing at all. You could be revealing the residual anger you feel at having been sitting on a delayed train to get to the event, or slight irritation because the chairperson has just pronounced your name incorrectly, or your concern that you have not yet spotted your supporter in the audience and, of course, a good, healthy dose of nerves.

The secret to successful NVC as you present is to let all of your enthusiasm show on your face and in your voice, which it will if you eliminate the negative NVC which can set in if you allow it to, and stress the positive NVC available to you. This is what we will be getting to grips with in the next chapter.

Eleven

USING YOUR NERVES

I have a vision of you, as you read the title of this chapter, snorting loudly in disbelieve that you could ever 'use your nerves'. I also imagine that, as you consider nerves in relation to a presentation, you might start to feel a slight tension in your stomach (which is good) and a rather unpleasant sense of doom (which is less good). I want you to feel nervous before a presentation – this is always a good thing. It means that you are alert to everything around you, that you are taking the occasion seriously and that you will perform at your best, but only if you learn to use your nerves rather than being ruled by them.

This chapter is divided into three sections:

- controlling your nervousness;
- using your nervousness;
- relaxation and breathing techniques, so that you can do both of these things.

Controlling your nerves

By controlling your nerves you will manage to avoid the distracting habits that presenters sometimes develop, but at the moment you might not know which habits you have already caught, as we tend to be unaware of them as we present. There are some common habits which trip up many scholars when giving papers or presentations:

 CHECKLIST

- **Fiddling:** If you know that you are likely to fiddle, take everything out of your pockets – playing with your loose change or your keys is noisy and distracting. If you tend to play with your hair, style it so as to make this more difficult than usual. Try to avoid picking up a pen or a pointer – you are likely to play with them, clicking at the pen and opening and closing the pointer.

- **Rocking:** This involves putting your feet almost one in front of the other and leaning forwards towards the audience and then backwards. It is such a common habit that it tends to be used in films where an old-fashioned head teacher is being depicted. We all know that rocking is comforting, it is why we rock babies, but it can unnerve an audience if you keep it up for any length of time.

- **Swaying:** This is similar to rocking, except that you sway from side to side rather than forwards and backwards. If you are wearing wide trousers or a flowing skirt this movement is particularly soothing, as the stroking of the material against your legs feels pleasant. As with rocking, this is distracting for the audience.

- **Rhythm:** Audiences seem to be fascinated by rhythm, watching, entranced, as the speaker, oblivious to what is happening, repeats an action time and time again. I recall once seeing a lecturer who spent the entire hour's lecture talking and unbuttoning his cardigan, then buttoning it again, then unbuttoning it and so on and so on. This was no mean feat – it was a thick wool cardigan, heather and moss green in colour, with large leather lattice buttons and buttonholes not quite big enough to unbutton the cardigan easily. The cardigan has stayed in my mind for 20 years; I have never had any idea what the chap actually said in the lecture.

- **Freezing:** This is a strange experience, and not one that you can do much about in its early stages, as you are unlikely to notice it happening. It begins with your calf muscles, which tighten up because you have forgotten to move in a while. Then your hips lock, but you keep talking, oblivious. When the freezing reaches your rib muscles you will start to notice that something is wrong, because you will not be able to breathe as regularly and deeply as you had been doing; you might also notice that you start using your hands to express yourself – your arms are about the only bit of you which has not yet frozen up. When the freezing gets to the point where you really are getting short of breath you will notice it – and panic. Although this is a rare experience, it is scary. Rather than panicking, immediately move your hips, slightly, sharply to one side. This will unfreeze you in a trice and the audience need never notice.

- **Hiding:** I mentioned this briefly in the last chapter. There are many ways to hide: sweeping your hand across your face for a moment's respite from the attention, turning to face the screen and failing to face back to the audience fully as you resume your talk; looking at just one person in the audience so that you can pretend the other audience members are not there. The main problem with hiding is that each presenter can find a new and unique way to do it. Working on your nerves so as to reduce your anxiety will help enormously; in the meantime, ask a supporter to watch you rehearse and to check whether this is a problem from which you suffer.

- **Lunging:** It is relatively rare to see lunging, but it can be spectacular when it does appear. The speaker starts to move forward a little towards the audience. If on a stage, the speaker might sit down on the front of the stage, perhaps for the Q & A session, before then standing in front of the stage. The creeping forward is almost imperceptible until the speaker is struck by a sudden thought, perhaps in answer to a question, at which point a lunge is made towards the audience.

Territory is always important in any public presentation. The speaker occupies a very specific space and the audience remains safe in another space, able to observe and interact but never forced to engage. By the speaker moving into audience space there is an instant sense of tension; the audience is likely to shut down as a result and be most reluctant to ask further questions. You may not have seen this happen at a presentation, but you might have noticed it in a meeting, where one member of the group is standing at the front and then leans forward on the desk or table to make a point; those members of the group nearest the front will instinctively move their chairs back if they can.

Avoiding this problem is best done before the event begins. If it is a small-scale, group situation, try to ensure that the seating is set up in such a way that there is clear space between you and the rest of the group. That way, you will have a visual clue as to territory. If you are speaking on a stage, and you know that you have a tendency to lunge, never let yourself sit on the edge of the stage or leave it altogether. If there is no stage and you know that you might drift toward the audience, you could consider placing a lectern or table between you.

With all of these potential problems you will need help to spot and then eliminate them. As you become more experienced and confident some of them might go of their own accord, although the habit might by then be entrenched. Rather than waiting, ask a supporter to watch you at an event with this list in hand, noting if you fall into any of these traps. Once you are aware of them, you can make a note every now and then on your prompts to remind you to avoid them.

Using your nerves

Nervousness can cause the problems I have outlined so far in this chapter, but it can also be used in a positive way to enhance your performance. In addition to the overall benefits of an increased, but controlled, level of adrenalin, there are five key ways in which you can use your nerves to good effect:

 CHECKLIST

- **Effective movement:** In normal, relaxed conversation, we have no need to notice most of the movements we make. We might lean towards someone in our enthusiasm, or turn sideways as we laugh, but we do this naturally. Because your level of awareness is heightened when you are a little nervous, you are in a better position to make some deliberate moves, giving useful cues to your audience.

You might, for example, deliberately take one step forward when you want to engage the audience's attention more fully at an important place in your presentation; you could turn resolutely towards the screen to indicate that you would like everyone to look at a new slide. These are not natural movements; they are exaggerated versions of what you might do normally. They are, however, an important part of your presentation style, important enough that I would always consciously include some of them in my rehearsals, to remind me that, at certain points, I will need to move in a very deliberate way. It will seem artificial to me, but the audience members will not notice; they will just follow my cue.

- **Productive gestures:** There was a time when presenters, at least in England, were urged to control their hands during a presentation, keeping them demurely in front of them and never using them to gesture in any way. The idea of 'flapping hands' seemed to fill some people with horror. This was probably never very good advice and is not something which would be advocated nowadays.

  If you naturally tend to use your hands to emphasise a point or enhance the flavour of your words, then use them in your presentation. Just make sure that your gestures do not become repetitive, such as wringing your hands, rubbing your palms together, 'steepling' you fingers or flinging your hand out in the same way each time you want to make a point. If you tend not to move your hands as you talk, try including a few gestures. This will feel strange to you at first, but your nervousness will help you remember to do it, and you will find that it can help you along if you occasionally gesture to the screen or board, or hold your hands out as you ask a rhetorical question.

- **Controlled feet:** I have already considered with you the importance of toe positioning in order to control your stance as you speak. We also need to consider your feet more generally. You never realise how large your hand is until you use it to screen your face from the audience for a moment (it easily covers most of your face); similarly, we never notice just how large our feet are until we are trying to work out what to do with them during a presentation or paper.

  You can ignore your feet only if a supporter has observed you perform and confirmed that you never do anything odd with them. 'Odd' here would include winding them around a chair or table leg, standing with one foot on top of the other, standing on the outside edges of your feet so that your instep is showing, standing on tiptoe repeatedly, assuming a standard ballet position. I have seen all of these, many times, so do not assume you are immune until someone has checked for you.

- **Making eye contact:** Shying away from your audience by making no eye contact at all is never going to work well in this situation. Even if you are giving a paper, and so looking down to read it for much of the time, you will still have rehearsed in such a way that you are in the habit of looking up frequently to make eye contact with those receiving the information. At the very least this will tell you whether they all look as if they are with you, rather than looking confused, and beyond this it will make the connection between speaker and audience which is so important to a successful event.

(Continued)

(Continued)

There are two ways in which you should *not* be making eye contact. Forcing your eyes to sweep the room, backwards and forwards, so that you roughly cover every part of the audience, is never a good idea. It induces the 'tennis effect' and it is clear to the audience that you are not actually engaging with anyone in the audience. Similarly, looking at a point just above the audience might feel like a good trick to you, but again the audience will spot within moments that you are looking over it rather than at the audience members.

An audience which becomes aware that you are using these techniques will disengage quickly, but making eye contact which is too prolonged will also cause difficulties. If you make eye contact with someone in the audience for too long (and this can happen without you realising it unless you make a conscious effort to avoid it) that person will feel uncomfortable. This is most usually evidenced by a nervous laugh or a frown of anxiety, as the person wonders why on earth you are staring.

So, you need to make eye contact in a natural way, properly engaging with members of the audience as you give your paper or presentation. This seems simple, but of course it might be the last thing you feel like doing when you are nervous. As your experience and thus your confidence grows you will find it natural to make eye contact quite spontaneously with members of even very large audiences, but this comes with time and you need a method that will work now.

I have found a way to do this that has served me well in the past, so you might like to try it out. I make sure that I arrive at the event early enough to meet a few members of the audience. When I am waiting to speak, I spot where they are in the audience so that when I begin to speak I can make eye contact with them first, knowing that they will smile at me encouragingly. Within seconds I am able to radiate out from each of them to increase the pool of people with whom I am making eye contact. That way the process looks natural and I can include everyone in my eye range very quickly.

 TOP TIP

Even when you have become very adept at talking to groups of people and making eye contact with them, it is still easy to miss out those people who, around a table or in an auditorium, are seated next or nearly next to you, or in the row in front of you but off to one side. This never seems to come naturally and you will have to develop the habit of deliberately looking to one side every now and then so as to make eye contact with them.

- **Smiling:** This gesture is such a strange thing. It is learned behaviour, coming to us several weeks after birth, and it can signal so many things. It can be a submissive gesture, accompanying giggling which is often a sign of surrender, or a nervous gesture, never really reaching the eyes, or a sarcastic signal of dismissal, or a sign of love, happiness or merriment. It can be any of these things, but one thing is for certain: it is one of the strongest mirroring NVC gestures we have. If you smile positively at someone it takes a ridiculous amount of effort for them not to smile back.

Many times I have begun a paper, or presentation, or lecture and I have genuinely smiled at the audience, keen to impart information and looking forward to the discussion that will follow. I would be lying, though, if I were to claim that this is always the case, yet even if I have no great enthusiasm for the task ahead, if my nerves are more taut than I would like or I am anxious about the reaction I might get, I would still take a moment to be silent and smile at the audience members before I begin. Why? Because I can guarantee that, without any conscious thought, they will smile back. My anxiety will be no match for the sea of smiling faces I am now seeing, and I will start in a more positive way than if I had not taken that moment. Indeed, I am so indulgent with the pleasure of being smiled at that I add the note 'SMILE!' to several of my prompts so that I can conjure up this boost throughout the event.

Relaxing and breathing well

The amount of time and effort you want to put into learning to relax and mastering breathing techniques might depend upon how badly you suffer from nervousness and how often, and in what circumstances, you expect to present in the years to come. What I will do here is to describe for you a breathing technique and a relaxation routine which work well and would be enough for most presenters. If you try them out, practise them and then use them a few times you will know whether they are enough for you – I expect that they will be. As these are techniques with which you are probably unfamiliar, and you will want to make the most of them as quickly as possible, I would suggest that you try using them in any stressful situation which comes up for you in the coming weeks and months; you do not have to wait for a presentation to get the benefit of them in action.

 EXERCISE

Relaxing in a heightened situation such as giving a paper or presentation is not going to feel the same as relaxing on your sofa or as you fall asleep. This is, rather, a sort of forced relaxation which can trick your body into a response which is predicated upon the assumption that you are calm and relaxed. This in turn leads to a relaxing of key muscles such as those surrounding your vocal chords and a reduction in excessive adrenalin.

1 Sit on a chair with the base of your spine supported, your knees a little apart and your feet solidly on the floor, below your knees.
2 Wiggle your toes to make sure that your feet and ankles are relaxed.

(Continued)

(Continued)

3   Rest your hands on your thighs, palms flat down, and fingers spread apart: it is quite difficult to be too tense when you cannot make your fist into a ball.

4   Now do one of two things: either relax your shoulders so that you can feel them dropping down or, if you find this hard to do, try elongating the back of your neck by tucking your chin down. This will have the effect of relaxing your shoulders – you must feel them positively moving downwards and/or getting less tense.

5   Raise your chin again if you have lowered it, and think about your tongue. Where is it? Probably stuck to the roof of your dry mouth if you are nervous. Make a conscious effort to bring your tongue down so that it is relaxed at the base of your mouth. By relaxing your shoulders and tongue you have released the muscles around your vocal chords so that you can open them up and speak well; you have also continued with the process of relaxing your body.

6   You now need to continue that process. Taking your right hand, press firmly with your fingertips at the top of your left shoulder blade, at the side of the base of your neck – there is a band of muscle between your neck and the bone.

7   Move across this muscle, towards your shoulder, pressing down firmly with your fingertips repeatedly as you go. If you are tense, this muscle could be very hard and it might be uncomfortable to press down on it.

8   As you reach the edge of your shoulder, move down the back of your left arm, using the fingers of your right hand to pinch at the muscle at the back of your arm. Continue right down to your wrist.

9   Repeat steps 6–8 using your left hand on the right side of the body.

10 Return to your original position and sit for a moment to get a sense of how your body feels. You should feel alert but not overly tense. You will certainly feel calmer.

One of the pleasures of this relaxation routine is that you can do it almost anywhere. If you consider it, you will realise that many of these actions are those that we do quite naturally when we are tired or feeling overworked. Most of this routine can be done as you wait in the audience to present; indeed, I have seen it done on the stage itself without anyone noticing what was happening.

 TOP TIP

When you practise this make sure that, even if you are interrupted, you go back and work on both sides of your body equally. If not, it can give you a headache.

 EXERCISE

To control your breathing you need to learn how to breathe well, from your diaphragm, so that you can gain two benefits: controlling the pace and tone of your voice, and reducing your adrenalin levels to manageable proportions. Sometimes presenters are advised to breathe deeply, repeatedly, in order to calm down. This could work, but it can be disastrous. Flooding an adrenalin-fuelled body with excessive amounts of oxygen can lead to light-headedness and a feeling of increased panic rather than calm. Instead, try a controlled approach to balancing your breathing:

1 Sit on a chair with your lower back supported, as in the relaxation exercise. There is no need to assume a particular position; not too tense but not slouched down is good.
2 Find your diaphragm – this is the large muscle which partly supports, amongst other things, your rib cage. If you place your hand at the bottom and between your ribs you should be in the right place.
3 Keep your hand flat on your diaphragm, holding it there gently rather than pressing.
4 Breathe out fully. There is no need to force this or work too hard: just breathe out as you normally would and then push it a little further, for a couple more seconds.
5 Close your mouth fully and firmly.
6 Wait until you feel an urgent need to breathe. You should have the sort of feeling in your head that you would get if you had stayed underwater for too long.
7 Now, simply open your mouth and let your body do the work. It sounds easy, but it can take a lot of practice. Your instinct might be to use your intercostal muscles (those around your ribs) to breathe in. These would help you breathe and make you feel better, but it would be a forced breath. Instead, try not to move your muscles in a deliberate way at all. If you can train yourself just to open your mouth and let your body take over, you will find that your diaphragm does the work for you. You will take a deep, calming breath which will support your voice for far longer and keep you calm.
8 You will know when you have mastered this form of breathing because, as you open your mouth, your diaphragm will seem to 'pop' out towards your hand. This might be a slight movement at first, but with practice it can become quite marked.

 TOP TIP

As with the relaxation techniques, this exercise can be done quite happily as you wait to speak. Breathing in this way three times in a row is said to induce a feeling of greater calm in most people for about seven minutes: plenty enough time for you to work through your introductory material and get into the heart of your paper or presentation. It also improves your breathing depth and rhythm more generally, so has a double benefit.

Relaxation and breathing techniques are no doubt helpful in preparing you to give a convincing and professional-looking paper or presentation. All of the preparation work you will have done to this point will also, of course, be of immense value in producing a polished performance which will help you to disseminate your material in the most beneficial way for what you hope to achieve.

It is also very helpful to be able to visualise the person you want to be as you talk to your audience. Some of this is about reminding yourself of what you are trying to convey and what you hope to achieve by speaking to this audience. However, a large part of it is simply reminding yourself of how your want to feel: nervous, of course, but not debilitated by it; well prepared but not so over-rehearsed that you have wrung the spontaneity from your delivery; most of all, eager to share your material and then listen to how the audience respond: it is to this that I will turn next.

Twelve
HANDLING QUESTIONS

With the prospect of a paper or presentation looming it is tempting to plan to keep your head down and get through the Q & A session as quickly and easily as possible. This approach might be alluring, but it is a mistake, as I hope you will discover in this chapter.

Throughout this guide I have tended to use the term 'Q & A', standing for 'Question and Answer', but this is not always the case. There are events where there is no Q & A session, or it might be that you will be sharing a Q & A session with speakers who gave papers or presentations before or after you. If you are giving a group presentation you might each have to be ready to answer questions. There are events where a presenter is asked to lead a discussion; in rare cases you will be leading that discussion on a paper you have submitted in advance, which will have been read individually by the members of a discussion group rather than being read out loud by you at all. If you are chairing a round-table or panel discussion the amount of information you give out might be minimal, and the questions will be used to spark debate rather than being answered by you alone.

 TOP TIP

If you are giving a group presentation, decide in advance who is going to be question leader and field the questions. That person will receive each question and decide which member of the group is best placed to answer it. Once it has been answered, if time allows, the question leader will ask if anyone else on the team would like to add anything. If anyone on the team wants to interrupt an answer or especially wants to be the one to answer a question, they will ask permission of the question leader before saying anything. The question leader needs to be someone who is confident enough to take the questions, strong enough to control the situation, and

(Continued)

(Continued)

dedicated enough to be aware of all aspects of the presentation so as to know who should answer a question. They must also be generous enough not to try to answer each question as an individual, but rather be prepared to pass the question unless it particularly relates to their section of the presentation.

The many possible variations in how the Q & A section of a paper or presentation slot is going to be handled makes the point, I hope, that you need to know to what you are committing yourself before you begin to plan and prepare for your talk. If you are being asked to lead a discussion, for example, you might offer some points for consideration on a handout to get things moving. If, on the other hand, you are given just five minutes of Q & A time you can safely assume that you will be expected to clarify a few points from your talk without expanding on them at any length.

 TOP TIP

Audiences are unforgiving on time in this context. You simply cannot go over on time, however fascinated you are by what is being discussed, however interested the audience seems. If you were introduced by a chairperson, glance across as the finish time for your event draws near; only take the next question if you receive a nod of encouragement. Ideally, the chairperson will let everyone know when there is only time for one more question. If it is obvious that a topic is going to run over the time, you could offer to continue the discussion over the next refreshment break. That way nobody will feel either abandoned without having fully made their point to you, or excluded because you did not get to their question.

Although you might quite sensibly be anxious to finish on time, you might be even more anxious at the very beginning of the Q & A session, as you wait for the first question. The few seconds in which you will be waiting for a question can seem like long minutes; you can easily become convinced that nobody is very interested, if they were even listening at all. Feeling like this is only natural, so take charge of the situation so that you can vanquish those negative thoughts. First, stay silent, smile encouragingly and resist the temptation to start talking. Questions will come if you are brave and wait for them. Second, do not let yourself be so relieved when the first question arrives that you spend far too long in answering even a very basic question. Instead, pretend to yourself that you have a line of questioners waiting behind this first one and answer the question only as fully as you need to. You will find that it will not actually have been a pretence at all: once someone has broken the ice more questions will follow.

There are distinct types of questioner you might meet and I have found that categorising them helps me to respond appropriately to each question. This saves me time and it also ensures that the Q & A session is productive. Note that this concerns questioners, not questions. Speakers sometimes dread a difficult question, but how hard, or unexpected, or off topic a question is does not matter; you would try to answer it, or ask the audience to help you to answer it. It is the questioner who can cause you problems:

  CHECKLIST

- the helpful questioner;
- the too helpful questioner;
- the neutral questioner;
- the aggressive questioner;
- the angry questioner;
- the questioner without a question;
- the confused questioner;
- the plant.

Although we are all individuals and each question will bring with it the nuance an individual places upon it, using these categories will give you clues as to how to deal with each type of questioner.

The helpful questioner: This might be the chairperson, who may even have prepared a question in advance so as to get the Q & A started. Helpful questioners kindly give you questions in which they have an interest, but which they also hope will be useful to you; the type of question which would allow you to expand easily upon one aspect of your talk, for instance.

Answer the question with enthusiasm – it is a gift of a question – but do not allow yourself to talk for too long. If anyone would like more information they can ask you another question in this area, but if you answer at length you risk other members of the audience feeling disgruntled because they might not have time to ask their question.

The too helpful questioner: Although full of goodwill and trying to ask you a question which you would enjoy, the too helpful questioner has a tendency to clarify the points in the question to such an extent that the answer is starting to creep into the question. Sometimes this person will be so keen to show that you have a common area of interest that the question becomes a little too much about the questioner. By the time the question is asked, there may not be much of the original query left unanswered.

Answer this in the spirit in which it was intended. Although your answer is likely to be quite short, perhaps little more than an agreement with what the questioner has already said, if you answer smilingly and with enthusiasm, maybe with a suggestion that you talk more later on, the questioner is rewarded for such enthusiasm and you can move on to more demanding interrogations of your material.

The neutral questioner: This is the type of questioner you would logically expect to be asking you a question, someone who would like clarification of a point, or who has been struck by something you said and would like you to talk about it a little more.

This question can be answered without any special concern. You simply need to identify what is being requested: is it clarification, or is it an expansion of a point which has been understood? This is the only aspect of a neutral question which can trip you up, so keep it in mind. As you answer the question, maintain eye contact with the questioner and the audience more generally; it is this type of question which can often lead to supplementary questions or a more general discussion.

The aggressive questioner: Presenters sometimes dread this questioner, but this is actually a relatively easy situation to handle, even if it does make you feel tense for a short while. You will hopefully pick up from the body language that this person is getting ready to challenge you. The question will come out without any hesitation: clearly the questioner has been thinking about it for a while. It will be a challenging question, but not necessarily impossible to answer – the problem is the questioner rather than the question.

The first thing to remember at this moment is that the audience is on your side. Members of the audience will no doubt have noticed that the question was asked in a bullish manner and so, as long as you do not make them feel awkward, you will be fine. If the question is one you had expected or that is easy to answer, go ahead and answer it calmly and fully, ignoring the tone in which it was asked. If it is about an area of your research on which you have prepared no material for the presentation, or it is a question to which you have no good answer, do not try to bluff your way through. Smile, thank the questioner for such a good question, and close things down as soon as you can. You can do this in three ways:

1. Say that you have no clear answer and ask the questioner if he/she has any thoughts on it? That way the onus is off you to answer and the questioner might be appeased if the cause of the aggression was a sense of grievance that he/she was not giving the presentation in the first place. However, you

will still have to keep control: if it looks as if the questioner is going to veer off into a lecture on the topic, look appealingly at the clock and then the chairperson, in case the chairperson would like to call things to order; if you do not get a response, look fascinated but interrupt the questioner, saying that whilst the two of you could probably talk all day about such an interesting area, you want to give the rest of the audience members a chance to join in. You can then suggest that you meet at some point to talk about the area some more. You have resolved the problem for now; you will have to be vigilant about avoiding this person monopolising your time for every break of the conference, but that is a relatively easy problem to handle.

2. You could take a similar tack by admitting that your research in this particular area of your chosen subject so far is limited, or in the early stages, and you would love to hear the views of other members of the audience. They will feel for you in such a tricky situation and will want to come to your rescue. They are also likely to have some interesting ideas to share, so you win in several ways.

3. If the question is not just difficult, but potentially damaging to what you are trying to achieve (such as something so off the topic that it will simply waste everyone's time, or a theory which you know has been discredited but would take ages to discuss and dismiss) or if the questioner is so aggressive that you find it intimidating, you can close it down without any discussion. A firm answer of 'That's interesting but no, I have never thought of that. Could I please get your email address later so that we can discuss it in more detail?' is usually enough to stop the questioner from taking it any further. If the questioner still comes back at you, clearly determined to pursue the question, you will have to be resolute and explain: 'Thank you, but I am conscious that we have a limited amount of time and this is such a niche area of my topic I am not sure how many audience members would have an interest. Can we discuss it over coffee?' If you look enquiringly at the audience you will get smiles and nods – followed swiftly by another question.

Remember, though, that these tactics will only work if the questioner is obviously aggressive and asking a question which is off topic, or an excuse to lecture you, or clearly something which you cannot answer. You will not get the same level of support from the audience if you try this tactic with every slightly tricky question.

The angry questioner: This is a slightly different type of person, one who is usually easier to handle than the aggressive questioner. The stance might be similar, but the chances are that the question will come out in rather a haphazard way; it might even be a little confused and difficult to understand. This questioner might be angry for all sorts of reasons, and they may have nothing to do with you. If you do not understand the question, be clear about this. If you ask for the question to be repeated, as if you did not hear it clearly, the questioner will get even angrier. If you admit that you are not sure you understood the question, this might help the questioner to calm down.

If you understand the question and it is answerable, the first thing to do is to smile resolutely at the questioner. This might bring the person around to realising that anger is inappropriate in this context; at the least it will disconcert the questioner, who will not be expecting such a friendly response.

Keep your reply brief and rather than asking the questioner if you have answered sufficiently, turn to the rest of the audience and ask if anyone else has anything they would like to add. That way you are diffusing the situation whilst still answering the question. If you cannot answer the question, do not bluff. In this situation, treat the angry questioner just as you would the aggressive questioner who asks an impossible question.

The questioner without a question: It is a most peculiar experience when this first happens to you, but it is quite common, especially in academia, so you need to be ready for it. An audience member begins to ask you a question, perhaps complimenting you first on a fascinating paper or presentation. You, quite naturally, feel positive about this question and kindly disposed towards the questioner. For a while. After half a minute you are a little concerned: when is the question actually going to be asked? You stay alert, listening out for any possible question in there, but there is none. After a full minute you realise that there will be no question: this person is simply giving a lecture about his or her own experience or expertise in your area of interest.

This may not be an awkward or aggressive questioner, so try to think back first to any NVC signs you noticed. If you did not notice the questioner, the chances are that this is just someone who is genuinely very interested in the topic and has become caught up in the moment, talking away without realising that there is no question. If the mini-lecture is fascinating, there is no need to stop it. If it is boring you, and boring the rest of the audience, then you might want to draw attention to what is happening by nodding vigorously, smiling and leaning forward as if to interrupt. This will often bring the questioner around to a realisation that this is supposed to be a Q & A session. This moment can be enjoyable. The audience will have been vaguely amused by the questioner, aware of what is going on and feeling no malice towards someone who is so passionate about the topic. Audience members might also be mildly intrigued to see how you will handle the situation. If the questioner comes back around and is a little startled, smiling and apologising for the fact that there has not actually been a question asked, everyone will smile and there will be goodwill all around, both towards you and the questioner.

However, if you noticed this questioner during your talk, and noticed obviously dominant body language, be wary. This is someone who loves to hear his/her own voice and is going to be determined to hold forth as long as possible. Being used to getting his/her own way in these things means that the lecture could take up the rest of your question time. If you notice a dominant or aggressive stance developing, or closed eyes (or a refusal to look at and engage with you) then you need to draw this interlude to a close. As with the aggressive questioner you can look at the chairperson enquiringly; you might receive a signal to let the person keep talking, or a nod that you should interrupt, or the chair might take on the task of moving the session on to the next question. Follow the cues offered by the chair and move things along as resolutely as possible.

The confused questioner: You have worked hard for this event and so it can be disappointing to have a questioner ask you something so banal as to suggest that your material has barely been understood and is certainly not being appreciated in all its wonderful complexity. Even worse, a confused questioner might ask you about something which you have already quite clearly said in your presentation.

In both of these cases your intention must be twofold: to dismiss this questioner as quickly as possible whilst demonstrating to the audience that you are an understanding and patient person, someone with whom any of them might like to work in the future. Never, ever give in to the temptation simply to say 'But I just told you that' or, no better, 'As I showed you on my first slide …' whilst, even worse, going back to the slide on the screen so that everyone can see the questioner's humiliation. Remember that the rest of the room is aware that you have already given out the information, and the questioner will probably also become aware of this as soon as you start to speak, so keep your answer as short and simple as possible.

I once gave a talk where the confused questioner was generous enough to stop me as I was giving the succinct but polite answer, to say that he was so sorry, he now recalled that I had said all this before, and he did not want to waste everyone's time; might he move on to his supplementary question? A brilliant question followed, a delightful lunch ensued, and we worked together on our next research project.

If your experience is not this pleasant, you are not stopped mid-answer and you have to repeat the material and then you are asked a supplementary question which is as confused and non-productive as the first, you can quite reasonably say that the question is not about an area of research you have been pursuing, but that you would be happy to contact the questioner in the future should you do so. This will usually suffice: confused questioners can be an irritation, but they are rarely persistent.

The plant: I have referred frequently in this guide to your supporters, those who might offer you feedback on your plan, or help you to perfect your first drafts of a presentation. They will be the friends and colleagues who are prepared to watch you rehearse and give an honest response to your efforts. The Q & A session might be the final task you set one of your supporters. If all else fails, and you have waited an inordinate amount of time for your first question, to the point where you are getting a bit panicky, or when you want to escape from a difficult questioner and are looking around the audience for another question, your supporter could be there, ready to ask that much needed question. This might be a question thought up as you talked, or one which you devised between you before the event.

This might seem like cheating, but it is not. If you have planted both the questioner and the question, you will have ensured that it is a question which is going to be of genuine interest to the audience. What you really cannot do is use your plant to ask a question just so that you can introduce more material of your choosing, material which you did not have time to include in the paper or presentation: this is unfair to the audience and will probably be spotted by some audience members.

Your plant will have to be well trained in the art of this type of question: rushing in too quickly could deprive another questioner of the chance to contribute and a question which is too lengthy or which requires a convoluted answer also risks wasting time which could be better used by another questioner. So, be clear in your instructions: the plant is only to leap into action if no questions at all are forthcoming after a significant amount of time or if you are trapped by an unreasonable questioner – this would be doing the audience a favour, as well as you.

 TOP TIP

If you are struggling to hear someone's question to you, it is fine to ask the questioner to repeat it. In such a public forum anyone would usually do this with great clarity, anxious to make you understand. If you still cannot understand it, look to those audience members sitting beside or near the questioner with an enquiring expression: they will feel compelled to repeat it to you. If you think that some audience members might not have heard a question, repeat it before you answer it, so that everyone is clear about what is happening.

Ideally every Q & A session should come to feel like a discussion; even if it is not really as free ranging as a social conversation, you will want to create the feeling of colleagues talking together about a subject on which everyone might have something to contribute. The easiest way to do this is to be methodical in the way you answer each question. Look at the questioner as the question is asked, and maintain eye contact until the very end of the question. Not everyone will be as adept at public speaking as you are, and they may stumble over the question or take some time to articulate their thoughts; they will then be irritated if you answer the question you thought they wanted to ask rather than waiting for them to finish. Once you begin to answer the question, turn very deliberately to face the whole audience, making it clear that your words are for everyone's benefit. Look out for a raised hand or other indicators that an audience member would like to add something to your answer.

If a member of the audience does contribute some material or an opinion to supplement your answer, this is a good thing: it means that you seem open to ideas and your talk was inspiring. However, you have to keep control of the time and the easiest way to do this is to thank someone, genuinely but firmly, when you feel that they have contributed enough for the time available. Once you have answered the question, or closed down the discussion on that area of your topic, look back at the original questioner to ask if you have answered the question fully enough. As well as looking courteous, this shows the audience that you are moving on to the next question. Only allow one supplementary question from the original questioner at this stage; anything more than this could be discussed over a break.

The meticulous way in which you have prepared your material, the structure which has led to some obvious areas for further discussion, even, perhaps the handout you have offered with some additional material: all of these may help to tailor the types of questions you receive. If you are asked something unexpectedly, you can remind yourself that you have acquitted yourself well so far and that you are capable of answering even unexpected questions fully and with spirit: this is, after all, your area of expertise. To receive a flurry of good questions from animated questioners is a huge compliment and a great reflection on all of the work you have put into this event: relish them.

Thirteen

POSTER PRESENTATIONS

Poster presentations continue to be a popular way to present information at conferences, both in a research and a commercial setting. Within academia, whereas once they tended to be in the preserve of the Sciences, they are becoming increasingly popular in the Arts and Humanities.

Why would I give a poster presentation?

They offer you several advantages:

- A poster forces you to display your material in a succinct and engaging way: this challenge can be useful in itself, helping you to clarify your thinking.
- Most of the dissemination takes place though the poster rather than through you talking; this can be an easy introduction to the conference circuit.
- The preparation for dissemination focuses on a static outlet, a poster, rather than relying on your ability to talk convincingly and accurately for a set amount of time.
- You might only be talking about your poster to a small group of interested onlookers, rather than a huge hall full of people.
- A poster lets you enjoy your creative side, which can be a pleasing break from your everyday activities.
- Selling your ideas to a group of colleagues or fellow researchers can sometimes be easier through written material and images than through a talk, however good your data projector slides.
- You can reuse a poster; indeed you can even send a PDF of it to interested parties after the event, or have it displayed with nothing more than your email address beside it so that anyone who wants to discuss it with you can come to you direct.

In case I have made the option of a poster presentation sound so appealing that you never want to do anything else, let me also share with you some of the potential pitfalls of poster presentations:

- You can only display a limited amount of information on even the best presented poster: you can often disseminate far more material by talking.
- Your time to speak is limited – perhaps to just a few minutes or to a series of questions and answers. This might initially be appealing, and it can be a very useful experience, but be aware also of this as a limitation.
- One simple spelling mistake will glare out at you from your poster, so your planning, preparation and proofing must be meticulous: there is no room for error.
- Producing a professional-level poster will cost you: not huge amounts perhaps, but having it produced by your organisations' design and print office, or via a print or stationery outlet, is going to incur some cost.

Where would I give a poster presentation?

There are some conferences which are simply 'poster conferences' so these opportunities are easy to spot. Also look out, though, for events which might include poster presentations but where they would be advertised less obviously. For example, a conventional conference might include a poster session, or a display of posters in one room, perhaps with poster presenters making themselves available at a specific time (perhaps over a break time) to answer questions about their posters. Look also for exhibitions and similar events which are not an obvious place for dissemination. If your work is funded by an external body, for example, a poster with an update on your project so far might be very welcome, whether or not you attend the event at which it is displayed.

Displaying your poster might need some lateral thinking, but it should be worth it. I recently attended a local art exhibition at which several scholars were displaying posters on their research into art history. It added hugely to the pleasure of the event and it ensured that they could tick plenty of 'impact' boxes around their research output.

What might the format for the event be?

Generally speaking, there are four ways in which a poster presentation might be given:

- The poster might be displayed with nothing but a name and contact email to one side of it, so that those interested in your poster material can get in touch with you.
- More usually, you will be beside the poster. For some events you would be asked to stand beside your poster at a set time, ready to answer any questions people have as they walk around the poster display area.
- Alternatively, you might be asked to stand by your poster with a seated audience in front of you. The audience will have viewed your poster in advance and there is now a Q & A session, where you offer answers to the entire audience. This session might move from poster to poster in terms of the questions asked or the questions might be fired at the poster presenters randomly.
- More akin to a full-blown presentation, you might be asked to 'speak to your poster', that is, give a brief presentation (five minutes or so would be typical) based upon the material on your poster. This may, or may not, be followed by a Q & A session.

 TOP TIP

Posters are sometimes grouped according to topic or subject matter. Take a look around at the other posters before you speak to your poster or answer questions. It always looks good if you can make a passing reference to the other posters on display in relation to what you have to say about your own.

How big should my poster be?

It is essential that you check this with the organisers, as a finite amount of space might have been allowed for the number of posters being shown. Posters might be flipchart size or, most usually, double that size, used in landscape orientation.

 TOP TIP

If you are being asked to speak to your poster, make a copy of it and put it on a data projector slide, or divide it up into a separate set of images which cover three or four slides, with an additional slide showing your name and topic area first, save it and have it somewhere to hand. It is sometimes the case that organisers ask poster presenters to speak to their posters from the other side of the room, so you would not be able to point out a particular section of your poster.

Should I use colour?

Almost without exception, the answer to this is yes. However, despite the fact that posters are intended to make a pleasing visual impact and so are almost invariably produced in colour, it is still worth checking this with the organisers. I once attended a poster display in a medical museum where all the posters were in black, white and grey, with maroon as the only accent colour. One presenter had clearly not checked on this and produced a beautifully coloured poster which in another setting would have been impressive; in this setting it looked oddly amateurish.

 TOP TIP

Although the choice of colour is, of course, up to you, I have found over the years that green, orange and purple lend the greatest impact to a poster.

Is there a font size or style I should use?

No, unless for some reason the organisers specifically ask you to do so. If you are speaking to your poster you can expect your audience to have seen it, and so have a rough idea of the content, but it would be unrealistic to point to a paragraph and expect that any audience member could actually read it as you talk. Instead, point in general terms to a section so as to remind your audience of roughly which area they need to recall. Certainly never rely on audience members to have complete recall of the material.

 TOP TIP

Poster presenters are sometimes disappointed that their poster looks messy, or is not as sleek and professional as they would like. This is rarely an issue of font size or style – although sans serif fonts such as Arial and Calibri tend to be clearer on the page – it is more usually a question of space. Allow enough clear space around the page so that the material can 'breathe'. It is better to have all of the viewers happily reading an entire poster of succinct information rather than cramming so much material on there that nobody wants to work through it all.

What about branding?

You will want to consider three possible branding issues:

- Does your organisation require you to follow strict branding conventions? These might include a logo or motif on your poster, using a certain font style, even perhaps dictating the colours you can use. It is vital you know about this, especially if you are hoping that your organisation will pay for the cost of producing the poster.
- Does the event have a list of instructions as to how the posters should be produced? These might include the logo for the event being included somewhere, for example.
- Would you like to set up your own personal branding? If you intend to give a series of posters over several events, or are likely to produce plenty of public material over the next few years, you might like to think now about whether you would like to choose layout conventions, a font style and size, perhaps a set of colours, which people might, over time, associate with you and your work.

 TOP TIP

If you have not had to think about branding before, a quick search under 'branding' or 'marketing conventions' on your organisation's intranet should tell you all that you need to know. We tend to forget that our organisations are more than just the place in which we live out our professional lives – they too have a life of their own and the sheer quantity of branding that comes as part of that life can be a bit of a surprise when you first come across it.

How much material should I include?

Plan your poster as you would a presentation. You can include the same number of main points on a poster as you would in a presentation; you just need to be ruthless about prioritising. Think about the overall function of the poster for you, and focus on that. This might mean that your first three points end up being no more than a series of brief bullet points, because half the space on your poster is devoted to two central points, with your final point included in a section entitled 'Further research questions ...' or 'Moving on ...'.

If you are not sure about how much information makes for a good poster, ask some friends or colleagues to look at it in the very early stages, perhaps when you have sketched a rough outline of it, to see if they instantly respond positively. If it is taking them time to work through it and they seem uncertain of the central points you are trying to make, be firm with yourself and reduce the content.

 TOP TIP

When I am asked to look at a draft of a poster I usually ask the poster presenter not to give me any background information (as I would not have this were I to be viewing the poster at the event) and to give me a copy of the draft poster on which I can draw. I then use a highlighter to put one word over each section of the poster, with my initial impression of the chief point being conveyed in that section. This seems to lend clarity to the process.

What if I have too much information?

Sometimes you can feel so compelled to communicate that it is painful to have to leave out information, however much you remind yourself that you want to produce an attractive and successful communication tool. This feeling makes it difficult to judge whether or not you might have too much information on there. An additional problem you have is that you may not be expected to produce a handout for your poster. If this is not encouraged, you would risk looking disorganised if you were to produce a handout simply in order to dump extraneous material somewhere.

I find that the method I mentioned above can be very useful here. When you have the draft poster in front of you, go back to your plan and look at your few main points. Designate just one word to each of these points, for simplicity, and then use a highlighter pen to put a word over each image and chunk of text on the poster. This way you will see whether one of your points has densely packed text under it: could you cut it down, or are all of these words needed? You can also see how dispersed, if at all, your points have become. If one point from your plan appears in six different places on your poster, you might want to think about whether you are losing the logical flow of information you need on a poster.

 TOP TIP

The balance between images and texts is important to the success of a poster. This is one way in which a poster might differ significantly from a data projector slideshow. On each slide, if you have beautifully laid out text which is simply and elegantly displayed, you might need no images at all,

(Continued)

(Continued)

whereas a poster would usually be expected to have images. The proportion of image to text varies from discipline to discipline and will depend also on your specific subject matter, but it is worth noting that, in a crowded poster display room, people tend to go first to the posters where at least 25 per cent of the space is taken up with images, either in the form of photos and artistic images, diagrams and graphics, or images suggesting a way to read the poster, such as arrows.

How do I lay out my poster?

Movement through a poster is always attractive, and helps the reader understand the way in which each section of your material relates to the other sections. If you are describing a process then a flow chart design would naturally reflect that process and bring a logical order to your poster. However, even if you are not in the easy position of relating a process, you can still introduce movement. This could be achieved in several ways:

- using arrows to guide the reader around the poster;
- dividing the poster up into sections, with each section effectively representing a 'chapter' in the story your poster is telling;
- using eye-catching images to draw the reader to each section of the poster;
- using any one of the many diagram templates available on your computer's standard software system to introduce a sense of order.

 TOP TIP

I have often noticed how easily viewers can lose their way around a poster. In the days when I first began helping people to plan and prepare posters the 'storyline' could be obvious to me, and to the poster presenter, but then when we asked supporters to check it we would notice that they seemed to have missed the importance of a point, or they had obviously read a couple of points in the wrong order. As a fail-safe, even if a poster is not concerned with a methodical process, I still urge poster presenters to introduce arrows or other movement indicators if they can, just to reassure the viewers that they are going in the right direction.

How can I edit my poster?

Producing a poster is a creative process, and you will naturally be pleased with the result once it is ready for proofing. Both of these factors make it quite difficult to edit or to proofread a poster effectively. I have already suggested that, if you have too much material on your poster, you go back to your plan in order to edit it down. I would also recommend that you do any finessing work on your poster on a large copy of it. Although you can work on it as you view it on your computer screen, or you could print it out in A4 size as you would a normal document, it can be hard to assess it effectively in these sizes. If you are trying to get an overview of the content, print it out in A3 size if you can; if you are thinking more about how well the layout and movement within the poster work, try printing out each section and laying it on a table top so that you can move the sections around until you are happy with their location.

 TOP TIP

When I am checking whether a layout works, and considering whether to edit the material, I print out a series of large arrows, so that as well as having sections I can move around, I also have the arrows I can place correctly so as to show how a viewer would move around the work. I would not always include arrows in the final product, but I do find them a useful tool as I edit.

How best can I proofread my poster?

When it comes to checking for errors on your poster, there are several techniques you could try:

- Print it out, in the largest size possible, in black and white. Colour can hide errors which become obvious in the starkness of black and white.
- Try reading through the sections in the right order first, and then immediately in reverse order. Expert proofreaders can read each sentence backwards, but for most of us just reading sections out of order is as much as we can do to spot mistakes.
- Copying each section into a plain text format and printing it out can help you to see it in a new light.
- Putting each section into a data projector slideshow, and then running through it as if you were about to give a talk on the poster, can help you to focus on any errors of content or structure.
- Leave as much time as you can between each proof check. The time lag will give you the chance to see it anew and you will more easily spot errors.

 TOP TIP

You might wonder why I have offered you five different suggestions on how you might find errors on your poster. It could seem a little anxiety laden to worry that much about the odd typing

(Continued)

(Continued)

mistake or misspelling. It is because the experience of standing in front of your glorious poster, ready to speak to an important audience, with every thought you want to share perfectly positioned in your mind, only to look and see the glaring error right in the middle of your poster is utterly demoralising. It also makes you look far less than professional. I would never countenance displaying a poster unless I had asked several people to check it for me, word by word.

How does a poster become a presentation?

The glib answer to this is that your poster will not become your presentation. It may be a simple answer, but it is nevertheless true. You will not be able to refer to the details on your poster during a presentation; you will only be able to gesture to an image, or the general direction of the material you are covering. This means that the poster itself is only a presentation aid in the most general sense. Added to this, it is unlikely that you would be able to cover all of the material on a poster in the few minutes you have probably been allowed for your presentation.

You also need to factor in the boredom threshold of the audience. You can safely assume that a significant proportion of the audience has looked through your poster before you present. So, if you simply repeat the material on your poster by talking through everything on there you could bore the audience; at best, people would be perplexed as to why they were being asked to listen to you when they had already read your poster.

Whilst you would not want to ignore whole sections of you poster, you will need to decide which section is to form the focus of your presentation, and then make this clear to an audience. For example, you might begin with:

> As you will have seen from my poster, my current research journey began when I visited Sweden four years ago [pointing to a picture on the poster]. I was struck by the cleanliness of the streets. This led me to wonder how a society can discourage anti-social behaviour such as littering, without imposing severe penalties [pointing to another section of the poster]. This led to a major research project, the latest findings of which I want to share with you today.

You can then follow with a few minutes of your presentation, for which you might not need to gesture to your poster at all. You could then spend the last minute of your presentation slot sharing with the audience the research questions which will lead to the next stage of your project; these might be noted in passing on the poster.

In this way your poster has supported your presentation and the poster and presentation become part of a whole as far as the audience is concerned, but your talk is succinct and intriguing, leaving audience members noting that they would like to look at your poster again and get hold of your email address before they leave.

 TOP TIP

As with any other presentation, plan to a little under the time you have been allotted – four minutes for every five you are given. Aim to leave the audience members wanting to know more rather than straining their patience by overrunning.

How do I use my poster after the event?

It would be a shame to waste any of the effort you have put into a poster by tucking it away and ignoring it after the event, especially as its usefulness is far from over. If you happen to have had a particularly tricky question about your poster at an event, or you feel that you did not present as well as you had hoped, try not to let this put you off the poster. Leave it to one side and then reassess it at a later date; it will impress you far more than you expect and you can then decide how to make it a useful resource in your dissemination plans.

There are several ways in which you might exploit your poster after the event:

- If you are asked to give another poster presentation and your poster is a general description of your research project it would be sensible to revise your talk but reuse your poster.
- I have already suggested that you will want to turn the poster into a PDF so that you can send it to anyone who expresses an interest; you might also like to ask for the PDF to be uploaded onto your organisation's website.
- A poster requires you to think about your research in an appealing yet precise way. If you focused on just part of a research project for a poster, consider whether you have in fact produced the kernel of a plan for a journal article: this can be an easy publication win.
- I have just spent an interesting five minutes staring at my computer screen having typed 'poster presentations' into an image search engine. It was pleasing to see so many happy presenters smiling beside their posters. If your organisation does not upload an image of your presentation, you might want to put it onto your own website or a searchable web space – assuming that you are happy for the world to see your material in this way.

- Having typed the last bullet point, I went to a video search site and used the same search term: it seems that posters provide many opportunities for self-publicity and, even if you do not enjoy the limelight, this is an easy way to get your work – and your name – into the public domain. All the usual provisos about the pitfalls of the internet would apply here, but it still needs to be considered as an option.

 TOP TIP

I once helped a postgraduate researcher from Canada to produce a poster about her research to date. She was due to present at a postgraduate conference I was arranging, at which research postgraduates at the end of their first year had been invited to give poster presentations. A month after the event I saw her and congratulated her again on her super poster. She beamed at me, telling me that she was thrilled with it, mainly because she had been able to display it at a family gathering the week before. She confessed that she had never found it easy to explain her research to her family, who wanted to support her but were unsure about the turn her life had taken. Finally, she was able to show them all exactly what she was doing. It is worth a thought …

Fourteen

MAKING THE MOST OF THE PRESENTATION OPPORTUNITY

Mastering the art of giving an impressive paper or presentation has necessarily filled most of the space in this guide, but it would be remiss of me not to mention the next stage in your development as a successful speaker: seeing beyond the immediate challenge so as to be able to take advantage of the wider opportunity opening up to you.

Look to the long term

Having already mentioned publishing to you in the form of a journal article, it is also worth keeping in mind that a presentation event is a useful place to hear about other people's plans. You might, for example, learn about a forthcoming collection of essays which is to be published and for which you could produce the perfect contribution. If the editor of the collection is at an event, this would obviously be someone you would like to meet. If your paper or presentation is, in effect, the essay you would like to contribute then your work is done for you, but if not, you will be able to use your talk as a showcase for the quality of the work you can produce.

 TOP TIP

It can be useful to you to keep a 'dissemination notebook' either in hard copy or online, in which you could note down ideas for papers or presentations, rough drafts, outlines and such like. That

(Continued)

(Continued)

way, nothing is ever wasted. When an opportunity arises you can look through the notebook to see if you have anything already in draft form which could be worked up into a successful paper or presentation for that particular event.

If the next stage of your research is reliant upon additional funding you will already be plugged into all the sources of new funding which might be open to you. What you may be less aware of are all the existing projects which have long-term funding and which might be developing in new and exciting areas – one of which could be just perfect for your interests. Take any approach from a scholar as a potential source of information about such things, as well as a pleasurable meeting with a like-minded individual.

Water cooler networking

Although this phrase was coined in America, it is a universally accepted concept in today's conference world. Chatting to delegates is pleasant, of course, but it is also useful in myriad ways. You might use the event to confirm 'warm contacts' – that is, individuals with whom you have been in contact before the event, and with whom you have arranged to meet. Conferences and similar events can be a very convenient way to meet your email correspondents for the first time, as well as catching up with friends and colleagues.

Cold contacts are also part of this type of networking. The most successful conference delegates are those who are prepared to give out a business card at a moment's notice and, more importantly, to ask for one in return. If this seems just a bit too businesslike for you, at least have a notebook and pen handy. Swap details with anyone whose work interests you, even if at that moment you cannot see why you might need to contact them in the future. I have often been grateful for the email address I jotted down, when weeks or months later I want to verify a fact and cannot think where I saw it first; one email can save hours of time spent in hunting down a source.

Online brainstorming

A network of contacts met at conferences, symposia and colloquia, or at research seminars, can be put to use straight away. You can achieve this easily by asking them if they would like to form a brainstorm group with you.

The idea is that any member of the group can email the whole group at any time with the outline of a particularly thorny research or project problem. The email should be no more than a few lines long, and the email group members will email back suggestions as to how the problem could be approached, drawing on their expertise and experience. Again, the reply must be just a few lines long so the process does not become too onerous and nobody tries to impose too much on anyone else's research. Over time you may well develop several of these groups, each covering one area of your professional life. The water cooler can be where it all starts.

Targeting your material

There has been no mention in this guide as to the subject matter of your paper or presentation beyond the dictates of your current research and what you can convincingly deliver in the time and format offered to you. Now, you might also like to consider the wider implications of the event. If you know that a researcher with whom you would love to work is in attendance, or representatives of a particular funding body will be there, or a publisher with a specialist output list is going to attend, each or any of these might have an influence on the content, scope and target of your paper or presentation.

 TOP TIP

Most speakers appear at conferences after a general call for papers, but if you are specifically invited to speak, be flattered and then ask why. It might be the case that either the organisers or a group of attendees have an interest in one aspect of your work, or a forthcoming publication upon which you are working.

Multidisciplinary opportunities and research groupings

It is only natural that most of your attention will be turned towards events in your own subject or discipline area, but also keep an eye on events in areas only tangentially linked to your own, as multidisciplinary opportunities can arise from them, leading sometimes to research groupings which are attractive to funding bodies.

Consider also events away from your normal dissemination forum. Public meetings, school and college lectures, tourist and leisure events, specialist society meetings: all of these can be useful arenas in which to share your expertise and your latest material. They offer you the opportunity to practise presenting and to sculpt your material for a new type of audience, they challenge you to find relevance and (dare I say it again) impact in your work, and they can be most enjoyable.

Your career

It might seem cynical to take an intellectual and personal challenge such as a paper or a presentation and then link it back to your career. For many of us, for much of the time, we are engrossed in and enjoying the rigours of our research and/or our latest project. The fact that what we do will end up on our CV may be far from our minds as we go about our everyday lives. This is probably as it should be.

Considering your career development is not necessarily going to improve your paper or presentation, but it would be a good idea, just once or twice in the process we have worked through together in this guide, to consider what you are aiming to do in the light of your career plans. For your professional image and your career goals, will the event, material, format and structure all serve your purpose best? I would not urge you to change the way you plan to do things just on the basis of how it might impact upon your career, but if you have a set of choices, such as which conference to attend, you might want, even once, to factor this aspect of your life into the equation before moving on firmly to areas of the challenge which will interest you far more.

Testing your material

We began this journey together with me suggesting to you that testing your material was one reason to present. As you have read through this guide, perhaps over some time as you prepare for a presentation and so work through each section, you will have felt a pull towards completion, a sense that you are committed to this and will persevere until you have produced an impressive paper or presentation. I hope that you have also felt a sense of freedom: the freedom to change your mind, indeed, the need to change your mind at any stage when things are not developing well. A willingness to change your mind in this context usually comes with experience and time, but I hope that this guide will save you some of that time.

If the event does not feel quite right for you, be prepared not to submit (or even to withdraw) your synopsis, outline or abstract. If new professional responsibilities arise unexpectedly as you are preparing, think about whether you could move your commitment to the event from a full-blown presentation to chairing a panel debate or giving a poster which you already have in hand.

Most importantly, if you begin to suspect that your material is not working as well as it should be, stop working on it. Remind yourself of what you are trying to achieve and re-interrogate your material in the light of this. If it might fail, go back to the planning and work through it all again. Some of the best conference papers I have heard have been those given by presenters who I know are prepared to discard ineffectual rough drafts and disjointed plans until they know that their talk will fit the bill.

 TOP TIP

Presenting your material is an emotional journey. Remain aware of this and do not finally discard plans, ideas, or rough drafts until you have given yourself enough time away so that you can come back and reassess them with a fresh eye before making a decision. Ideally, discuss your decision with a supporter before making a final choice about the best material, structure and so forth.

Testing yourself

It is easy to see a paper or presentation as a test of some kind, one in which you have to prove that you can tame and disseminate your material, pro-duce perfect presentation aids and master your performance. To some extent this is true, but the test is far more fundamental and subjective than this. You can do all of these things and you will have given a good talk. You will be pleased with the response to your performance, but the greatest pleasure lies in the personal and professional pride you can take in the fact that you conquered and then used your nerves, that you were the one to spot the call for papers and you took the time to go through the process; you worked and reworked your material until you had a permanent record of your work and were able to share it with others. In short, you managed to achieve all of this from doing what, having read this guide, you might be just about to do: take the plunge. I hope one day to see you on a speaker's platform. You'll know me – I'll be the one smiling as I spot you wiggling your toes as you start your relaxation routine.

INDEX